PLEIADIAN

PROPHECY

2020

The New Golden Age

James Carwin

Table of Contents

Introduction

Hello and thanks in advance for reading my book. My name is James Carwin, born February 5th, 1987. It is my honor to share the messages I have received from my spirit guide over the course of three years. The information compiled in this book are messages that I received through automatic writing, also known as channeled writing. Automatic writing is a form of mediumship or divination in which a psychic medium conveys messages from the spirit realm by allowing a spirit to guide or direct his handwriting.

I am not a psychic medium per se. My channeling sessions were made possible thanks to the use of a psychedelic substance that I prefer to leave unnamed. I was first introduced to this psychedelic in 2012. Instantly, I underwent a profound spiritual awakening. I remember feeling intense euphoria and a sense of spiritual connection with nature and all things around me. I've been using this substance periodically ever since.

My first time meeting my spirit guides occurred in 2013. I was deeply immersed in the effects of this psychedelic and, having done some research on the spiritual experiences other people have had with it, I attempted to make contact with my spirit guides. It was a fascinating concept for me, the idea that we all have spirit friends or guardians that guide and protect us throughout our lives. It took several sessions of meditative practice, but on one special evening, I managed to perceive what looked like an African-American woman standing beside me. I remember she had a warm, compassionate look in her eyes. She told me her name, but I was unable to hear it clearly. After more sessions of mediation under the use of this special substance, my connection improved and I was able to communicate much better with my spirit guide, whose name is Tinah.

After meeting Tinah, I become obsessed – I bought tarot cards, a Ouija board, a crystal ball, several books about contacting "the other side," anything that could help me facilitate a stronger connection with my spirit guide. When my connection with Tinah finally became crystal clear in early 2014, she and I had many engaging conversations. At first she told me about her life as a slave in Louisiana during the 1800s, where she secretly gave psychic readings to assist others before she was caught and killed for it. She also introduced me to other spirit guides of mine, one male who died in war and another female who is my great, great grandmother. I learned of their backgrounds as well, but remained mostly connected with Tinah.

I asked her about many things pertaining to my personal life. I quickly learned about the "Law of Attraction," how the power of our minds and emotions are the creative force behind all the experiences we have. I also learned about "The Law of One," how there is only one being in all of Creation and that everything in Creation is a different version of this one being. I also learned about destiny, the decisions and agreements we make before we incarnate and the life path or life themes we choose to explore before we are born. I began to ask her questions beyond my personal life, into the global reality of things, and then eventually, I began asking her about galactic and universal matters. For this, she felt rather inadequate, so she introduced me to a more suitable teacher – my Pleiadian guide, Deltavash.

Deltavash is an extraterrestrial being that comes from the star cluster we know as the Pleiades, approximately 400 light years away from Earth. She resides in the 4th dimension. It is generally believed among metaphysical teachers and students that our universe has 12 dimensions; different layers or planes of reality. The higher up you go in the dimensional ladder, the less physical or solid you become and the more connected you feel to everyone and everything around you.

My first conversation with Deltavash was so unforgettable and exciting! I felt a vibrant, electrical atmosphere in the room that I had never felt before as she began to write messages through me. At first I was unsure if she was visiting me in astral form, traveling thousands of light years just to speak to me. Later, she informed me that she was not traveling at all but communicating with me telepathically while still operating her physical body back home in the Pleiades.

Deltavash does not live on a planet. She lives in a giant spaceship that is almost the size of our moon! This spaceship is the mothership that carries most of the resources used by her people. There are large facilities for scientific work, animal husbandry, physical training and activities, and so much more on this spaceship. She told me that it began as a naturally-formed moon with land and a few bodies of water. It was later reconstructed to accommodate the space travel needs of her people. After introducing herself and her world to me on that warm summer day in 2014, a whirlwind of universal knowledge came flooding my way.

Most of the messages I receive through automatic writing do not come to me in complete sentences. I receive mostly the key words, the highlights or main points of the message, often as one or two-worded answers. For example, when I asked her about her home planet, she responded with the words "No planet. Spaceship. Moon." Therefore, I had a lot of editing and revising to do with writing this book in order to stretch out the channeled material into complete sentences. Some of the channeled messages are also quite random, jumping from one idea to another. I would also like to point out that all information gathered from Deltavash is filtered through my mind. Therefore, my own personality and personal beliefs are partially imprinted on these messages, though I try to be a clear channel as best I can. And so without further ado, here begins the journey into the wondrous messages of my Pleiadian guide...

The Pleiadian Alliance

Deltavash: Greetings, Jamie. What a great joy to finally be present with you! I am eager to begin our conversations. My name is Deltavash. I am a member of The Pleiadian Alliance, one of many interplanetary alliances that exist within the Pleiades. Some alliances are composed of only two or three planets. Our alliance is currently composed of 43 planets, making us the largest, but not the oldest grouping within the star cluster. There are much larger alliances that exist, some composed of thousands of worlds that span the entire galaxy and beyond. Some of these groups are interacting with humanity right now as we speak.

Each alliance has its own agenda. The Pleiadian Alliance is aimed at uplifting the galaxy. We attempt to achieve this by educating and defending civilizations that are in need of healing. Earth is merely one of thousands of worlds that require assistance in elevating to a positive status.

The Pleiades are a vast cluster of stars comprising a wide range of life forms. Many animals from Earth exist in the Pleiades as a humanoid or more intelligent version. There are intelligent species of birds, canine, reptiles, insects, and even marine creatures that exist in the Pleiades. Our alliance includes several types of these species and many more.

The general alignment or orientation of the Pleiades is one that is predominantly positive and loving in nature. Every star system has its own general alignment or orientation. If one was to gauge your solar system and the Earth by analyzing the general energy of its location, one could say that it is predominantly negative. Even though there are very loving and nurturing beings within the Earth locality, the negativity of your region outweighs the positivity. It is therefore appropriate for beings to label your world as a negative one. Conversely, there are some very dark and sinister beings in the Pleiades, yet the positivity of our star cluster outweighs the negativity. We are therefore regarded as a generally positive system, one that complements and offers much-needed compassion and spiritual wisdom to your world.

From our perspective, your solar system is about 40% positive. The Pleiades, on the other hand, is approximately 70% positive. The

Pleiadian Alliance is very much aligned with the generally themes and status of the Pleiades, though we must inform you, there are other alliances that are not. Some alliances have an opposing agenda and attempt to hinder our work.

I myself am what you could refer to as a birdwoman. Just as you humans are a humanoid and more advanced version of apes, my race is a humanoid and more advanced version of birds that somewhat resembles the hawk from your planet, in terms of our features. We have a similar range of emotions and intellectual capacity compared to you. We originated from the Carian star system. A small faction of Carians migrated to the Pleiades thousands of year ago, and this star cluster has been our homeland ever since. There are many legendary stories and depictions of bird people in your ancient writings and drawings. Some of these legends spawned from interactions between Earth and the Carians many years ago.

My race comes from a binary star system that lies behind Electra from your view. The name of our home star is Vormuda. There are three planets that are habitable to my race in this star system, and we occupy all of them. My ancestors were colonizers. When they first entered this star system, they began living on one planet and eventually conquered the remaining two, which were previously occupied by an intelligent race of amphibians.

I have lived many past lives throughout the galaxy. I have witnessed and experienced the tribulations of war in nearly every capacity. My race underwent a spiritual transformation after losing hundreds of innocent loved ones at the hands of a malicious insectoid race. Their invasion was not successful, but the experience taught us many lessons about suffering and the value of life. When the battles ended, we sought greater military might, greater protection, and greater spirituality. Eventually, we learned that the insectoid race of invaders had been subdued by fleets of The Pleiadian Alliance, and promptly we requested to join them.

Though I am Pleiadian, it is important that you understand the diversity of civilizations and personalities that come from the Pleiades. We are not all angelic beings of love and light, as many people on your planet come to think. There are both benevolent and malevolent, as well as neutral beings that come from the Pleiades. I myself belong to a soldier class within the military faction of The

Pleiadian Alliance. Therefore, I do not consider myself to be angelic at all, for I do enjoy the thrill of war and destruction. I can be mischievous and sometimes too snarly to fit the stereotypes that are often associated with Pleiadians. I regard myself as being half-way between positive and neutral for these reasons. Though The Pleiadian Alliance itself is predominantly positive, we do have some members that identify as neutral, and a few who are even somewhat lower than neutral. All beings within our alliance serve a purpose.

This is why I chose you, Jamie. You are an objective thinker with an open mind that can comprehend a wide range of ideas without bias or judgment. I knew we would be a perfect match, and it delighted me to connect with you when you began practicing automatic writing. Though I am a physical being, I can astral project and operate as a spirit whenever I wish. I am one of your spirit guides and I understand that your primary guides have turned you over to me since I am more adept at answering questions regarding universal matters.

Universal Knowledge

I wish to begin my teachings with a few general statements about the universe. First let me say, we live in a universe that exists within a greater multiverse. Creation encompasses an infinite number of universes. There are some universes that are sheer heaven or sheer hell by design. Our universe is one of duality, and thus, both polarities of dark and light are supported. This is represented by the male and female polar opposites that exist. Males represent the ego, which is service-to-self. Females represent the heart, which is service-to-others. Each individual carries a unique spiritual blending of male and female aspects. Some beings are in balance, some are not.

In general, our universe is currently out of balance. There is an overabundance of beings who operate exclusively from the ego, which we define as self-love. When an entity has love only for the self and no love or care for others, this creates a very negative consciousness that seeks to interact with others purely for personal gain. The ego chakra dominates a substantial portion of consciousness throughout this sector of the multiverse, effectively plunging countless souls into never-ending warfare. There is much healing that must be facilitated before a more harmonious experience for all can be established.

The Pleiadian Alliance has discovered that all things within the universe are interconnected through webs of energy. If you can imagine a cosmic web of interconnecting strings and points, imagine all of these webs eventually meeting at a single point – your solar system. The Earth is a nexus planet, one of many nexus points that energetically link a vast number of realities together. Like a biological organism, the universe is sustained by vital "organs" that keep it alive. You can think of Earth as the heart or brain of the universe; without it, the universe would die.

Just as your body has several chakras or energy points, the universe itself has its own chakra centers as well. Earth is located on one of the main and most critical chakra points of the universe. By altering this nexus, one has the potential to alter the entire universe. For this reason, we refer to Earth as the Crown of the Cosmos.

The discovery of Earth as a nexus planet comes from the future. There are many extraterrestrial groups that come from 300 years in your future and have traveled back in time in order to prevent something unspeakable from happening. Many groups who have witnessed a very dark, catastrophic turn of events. When the origin of these events was researched and analyzed, all of these groups came to the same conclusion and managed to trace the source of this evil back to your solar system. They have since evacuated their apocalyptic, native parallel version of the universe and migrated to your timeline. There are many versions of the future, of course, many different paths you can walk, but in all timelines or parallel universes, what happens to humanity affects the entire galaxy and eventually ripples out to the cosmos. What we and many other alliances are attempting to prevent, in cooperation, is the possibility of a universal apocalypse.

You humans are a very well-known race of beings throughout the universe. There are literally billions of beings from all corners of the universe, and especially from this galaxy, who are attracted to the Earth realm due to its ability to rewire the universal matrix. You can think of the Earth as the famous Excalibur from your legendary fairy tales, an object of great power sought by many. There is literally a race and a tug of war happening in space over your planet. The forces of light wish to uplift humanity. By doing so, we can help uplift the rest of the universe as well. On the other hand, the forces of darkness wish to increase the oppression. If they succeed, the universe may never experience healing, and all the warring and corruption that exists within it may only intensify.

Fortunately, the probabilities are in our favor. Humanity is approaching a crucial moment in time. Your timeline is a mixture of many different timelines existing simultaneously, like railroad tracks running parallel side by side. This is why Earth is both heaven and hell, a place where the best and worst experiences can be had, all contained within a singular bubble reality. You are rapidly approaching what we refer to as the Splitting Prism of Time.

Between the fall equinox of 2016 and the winter solstice of 2017, the parallel timelines will begin to literally split apart. Many great and positive changes will unfold on all fronts of your society. The negative aspects of your reality, in general, will begin to gradually diminish, so that no later than 2027, only the most positive timeline will remain, that which we call Alpha Earth. We members of The Pleiadian Alliance are here to prepare you for this auspicious splitting of realities and the exhilarating adventures that are sure to follow thereafter.

For the record, our main objective in communicating with you is to instill excitement, to propel the energy fields of those who receive our message towards a positive timeline on the universal scale. The more intent you put behind a positive outcome, the more likely it will manifest. Our teachings are intended to inspire your excitement, to make you enthusiastic about being alive on Earth at this time and to provide a glimpse of the probable future that our combined willpower can co-create.

We are honored to be in contact with you. It is akin to mentoring a chosen warrior in training before he ventures off to become the legendary champion of the world. This is indeed our prophecy for you, humans. Our vision highlights you as the Phoenix Planet, the version of Earth that is destined to rise from the ashes in a brilliant supernova of cosmic proportions. Only the bravest souls dare to participate in the most epic of journeys, such as the story of Earth. Your struggles will be greatly rewarded with levels of consciousness beyond anything ever witnessed in the history of the universe.

Though now you look up to us, the Pleiadians, for guidance and for wisdom, we assure you, dear friends, it is someday we that will be looking up to you.

-Deltavash

Secrets of the Universe

Our shared universe is one of countless others within the greater multiverse. Some universes are very similar to ours (you can think of them as our siblings or cousins) while other universes are radically different. The imagination is infinite, and thus, so too is Creation. Every imagining exists in some tangible form somewhere within the multiverse. Consciousness contains the ideas, the thoughts, the building blocks behind every reality. Sentience, on the other hand, is the creative force that animates reality and experiences all possible emotions and sensations within them. Consciousness creates reality, sentience experiences reality. Together, consciousness and sentience create the totality of Creation.

The Creator, what some of you call God or Source, is a neutral being. It is both male and female, thought and feeling, dark and light. The Creator is on an eternal journey to experience all possibilities. Every concept or idea that spawns from the infinite imagination of The Creator is destined to be experienced. This includes the greatest concept of heaven, the worst concept of hell, and all variations of realities in between. Through us, the souls throughout the multiverse, The Creator gets to experience itself. The Creator is you.

One common element within the multiverse are the polarities of pleasure and pain. Ultimately, no matter what reality you find yourself in, your experience will either be a pleasurable one or a painful one. There is also the neutral state in the middle which can be the combination or lack of both. It may surprise you to know that pain does not exist in some universes. These positive universes only support beautiful experiences. The denizens of such realities spend most of their time shifting from one flavor or degree of pleasure to another. Some regions of our universe operate in a similar way. Conversely, there are some rather negative universes in which pain is the most prominent sensation. These hellish universes are typically ruled by a minority of sadistic souls who use the majority of souls as food or slaves. Some depictions and illustrations of heaven and hell are actually visions of other universes that have seeped into human consciousness and translated into your art and literature.

Rest assured that the beings who live in hellish universes do not suffer forever. There is no such thing as eternal damnation. Creation is not biased. It honors the will of all beings equally. If you find yourself in a state of great pain and you wish to be free of it, you will. There may be a time lag, but your will is always honored by Creation. It may take hundreds or thousands of years to reach the healing or freedom you desire in some cases, but inevitably the time will come. It is a known truth throughout your world as well as the Pleiades – time heals all wounds. Remember this.

You are currently experiencing mass sacrifice on your planet. The majority of humanity has agreed to sacrifice itself for a minority of beings so that this minority can feel powerful or god-like by comparison. Power is always relative. You may believe that these beings which your conspiracy circles have come to call the Draconian Reptilians or the Illuminati are some almighty force that governs every aspect of your lives, but in actuality, you will be surprised to know that the power level of this minority is infantile compared to other beings that exist outside your planet. No one is ever inherently more powerful than anyone else. That which outshines you in one lifetime may become a speck of dust beneath your feet come the next.

We want you to understand the nature of lifespans on your planet. You do not incarnate into one reality, into a single lifetime and then leave. Like The Creator, souls throughout Creation are inquisitive. They want to experience realities from as many different points of view as possible. Think of a classical town and all the people in it: the farmer, the blacksmith, the mayor, the maid, the waiter, the outlaw, the police officer, etc. Each individual has a unique perspective and experience of that town. In order for one soul to experience reality from all these different perspectives, it can take many, many lifetimes. This is why we wish to tell you, when you decide to incarnate into any reality, you do not limit your experience to a single lifetime, a single generation, or even a single century. You incarnate into the ages! Your may have hundreds of physical lifetimes that last for about 70 years each, but your spiritual or "divine lifetime" on this planet is one that lasts several thousands of years.

Many of you believe that one age on Earth equates to one precession of the equinoxes which lasts about 26,000 years. From our perspective, one Earth age, one cycle through what your Hindu philosophy calls the Yugas is actually about 50,000 years long. Most of you have been here for that long, some of you have been here much longer. This span of time allows you to experience the Earth reality from many different points of view as you don a new identity, a new perspective with each new lifetime. This does mean, humans, that most of you have been both hero and villain, both predator and prey, both powerful and powerless. We assure you, however, that whatever karmic ties bind you to those you have interacted with in negative ways during this age will come to a balance point and be cleared in perfect timing by the end of this 50,000-year cycle, which you are on the verge of completing.

It is important for you to understand that our universe is neutral. Meaning, it supports both positive and negative experiences equally. Take a look at your body. Your state of being always begins in a neutral state. The body itself contains the support system for both pleasure and pain within it. This does not mean that pleasure and pain are equal. Pleasure, or positivity, is far more common throughout existence. Pain, or negativity, on the other hand, is contained to a minority. The two polarities are always in balance, however. You can think of positivity as a giant, brilliant star and negativity as a black hole – the star is much larger than the black hole, yet they are both equal in mass and can therefore orbit around each other in perfect balance.

Our shared galaxy, which you call the Milky Way, is an enormous cluster of solar systems that orbit around a central supermassive black hole. The supermassive black hole is billions of times smaller than the rest of the galaxy, yet the galaxy orbits around the black hole in perfect balance to create a singular body. The same basic concept applies to good and evil. There is a greater amount of good throughout Creation, yet the lesser amount of evil is potent enough to keep it in balance.

The majority of souls live in realities that are generally positive, however our particular universe has experienced something very unusual. It has come to the attention of The Pleiadian Alliance, as well as many other groups of extraterrestrial and extradimensional beings, that our universe's dark side is gradually increasing and overwhelming the light side. Going back to the previous analogy, the "black hole" has begun to grow bigger, overwhelming all the light surrounding it and is currently in the process of consuming it. Our universe is growing darker and darker with each passing day, and only with your assistance, humans, can we put a stop to it.

The origin of this phenomenon can be traced back to the birth of our universe. Our shared universe is trillions of years old. Your science claims that the "big bang" occurred approximately 14 billion years ago. This is correct. However, this is not the first big bang that has occurred. We are currently existing in the ninth birth/death cycle of the universe. The universe, as you all know, is expanding. Eventually, the momentum that is driving this expansion will run out, the gravitational pull between galaxies will draw everything in the universe back together, and the big bang phenomenon will occur all over again. This process of expansion and contraction has repeated nine times, and it will repeat again. We will share a brief overview of the universe's history as we know it. The information we are about to share is based only on the previous 14 billion years, even though the universe itself is several eons older.

The First and Second Phase

In the first phase of the universe, only nature existed. The Creator experienced itself only as basic matter: the stars, the planets, the galaxies, and the particles, atoms, and molecules that formed them after the big bang. According to the laws of physics or "rules of the game" of the universe, these particles would interact with each other to coalesce and form astronomical bodies. The Creator played with the formation of many different astronomical objects and the interactions between these objects.

All things within the universe hold consciousness and sentience. This is true for the grass you walk on; it can feel your footing. This is true for the air you breath; it understands itself as hot, cold, dry, humid, etc. Though it appears to most of you that basic matter is soulless and unfeeling, there is actually some degree of life within all things.

In the first phase, if a spirit wanted to experience the material world, it would merge its consciousness directly to the solid objects created by the universe – the stars, the planets, the comets, etc. These objects contain consciousness, and just as you can reincarnate as a bee, a whale, or a snail, so too can you experience reality from the point of view of a star. You can experience yourself as anything you can imagine.

Nothing in the universe happens by accident. Everything is intentionally created by the will of spirit consciousness which animates all things in Creation. Without consciousness, without ideas and inspiration, without intent and willpower, there would be no motion or activity in existence. What may appear random to you is always the intentional result of a spirit being's will.

In the second phase of the universe, life forms began to grow in more complex designs. The arrival of microbial organisms, as well as plant life and some forms of animals emerged within this phase. Basic matter would coalesce into structures that were much more intricate and organized. This was a very exciting time. Spirits could now experience the physical universe from perspectives of higher consciousness. These life forms were much more sociable with each other, and their level of sentience offered a higher capacity for sensations of joy, as well as fear. This phase set the foundation for even greater, more complex life forms to emerge.

The Third Phase: Dawn of Science

The third phase of the universe is where things began to go awry. The first wave of third-level consciousness emerged at this stage. You, as humans, currently exist as third-level or third density beings. It was at this level of physical intelligence that the corruption of the universe began to occur, 7 billion years ago. Once a being reaches third-level consciousness, they gain enough self-awareness to question their existence and the world around them. They are then able to understand their surrounding reality in such a way that they can then manipulate it.

The beginning of "science" occurred at this stage. People studied and learned the laws of physics, they analyzed and experimented with particles, molecules, objects, life forms – everything. After billions of years of research and practice, they eventually gained the ability to develop cities, spaceships, worm holes, as well as new life forms altogether. The study and understanding of matter and energy (nature) is called science. The manipulation of matter and energy to alter or create new products within nature is called technology. We refer to the third phase of the universe as the technological phase for this reason.

As the third phase grew, the novelty of technology incited great curiosity and adventure. People began creating and indulging in biological bodies that were designed to experience a wide variety of sensations. It became very popular for spirits to merge their consciousness with biological bodies for physical pleasure. As more and more souls became addicted to the wonders and pleasures of the flesh, they lost touch with their spiritual essence. Greed and self-serving behavior began to surge. When enough souls lost their way in physical reality and succumbed to materialism, wars began to break out.

War in itself became another exciting novelty. Carnivorism became another addictive novelty as well. The concepts of predator and prey, master and slave, the experience of winner-takes-all became heavily pursued by countless souls. Our universe, especially the lower dimensions of physicality, became realms of conflict and survival. For most societies, peace had to be earned by having strong defensive resources.

To this day, dear friends, there are many, many souls who are still immersed and addicted to physical, materialistic pleasure. They indulge in the abusive manipulation of nature to wield powerful technologies, and they revel in the domination of various worlds through war and conquest. Fortunately for us and countless others who have grown weary of constant fighting, the third phase of the universe is almost at an end. Guess what, dear friends? The novelty is beginning to wear off.

From our perspective, this entire phase of technology, manipulation and war has been nothing more than the theme of one time cycle. Just as your Earth moves through cycles of time, so too does the universe have cycles of its own. Over the last 7 billion years, more than 50% of the universe has become negative. This overgrowth of negativity is continuing as we speak, yet the rate of growth has begun to decelerate. This is exciting news! It shows we are making progress. Though there is still a long way to go before our freedom is guaranteed, we can confidently say that the future looks promising.

The Fourth Phase: Return to Balance

The fourth phase of the universe is the healing phase, though this is not yet guaranteed. If we can succeed in altering the frequency of the Earth location, the central chakra or nexus of the universe, and permanently establish it into a platform that is more conducive to positive expressions of life and consciousness, then the rest of the universe can feel its effects as well. By healing the Earth reality, we can succeed in bringing the rest of the universe into balance. This of course will only be the first step; it will require billions of years to "clean up the mess" left behind.

We are not saying that the entire universe will become a utopia. What we can expect is more of a balancing between the positive and negative forces. We can expect a decrease in materialism and war, and an increase in spirituality and unity. By making adjustments to the nexus points within the universal matrix, we can adjust very fabric of spacetime and the type of frequencies that it supports. It is our goal and the goal of many other beings to return this universe to what it was meant to be – a free will universe, where war and slavery are not a constant threat.

What you must understand is that your physical dimension affects everyone in the higher dimensions as well. All things are interconnected. All things are One. Therefore, if one dimension is broken and out of balance, then all other dimensions will experience repercussions. The universe is a singular body in itself, and just as cancer can spread from one portion of the body to all other surrounding areas, so too can an entire universe succumb to the untreated infection of a single dimension.

In many books and teachings throughout your world, you are told that Earth is the most hellish planet in the universe. Dear friends, allow us to be frank with you – your challenges are infantile compared to other places. There are species and societies through the Milky Way galaxy alone that experience a far deeper degree of suffering that any living creature on your planet. Suicide, for example, is a common cause of death on your planet, yet it is not nearly as prevalent as it is on other worlds. Some beings experience a degree of suffering that is so great, their entire civilization is suicidal.

That does not automatically mean they have the freedom to commit suicide, however. Despite their compelling desire to end their misery, their overlords make sure they cannot. These beings are so heavily controlled that even the idea of suicide is not allowed to cross their minds.

Suicide, in some cases, can be a luxury. It is a luxury on your planet because not all beings in existence who wish to end their pain are allowed to. We are not condoning any acts of suicide. We are merely highlighting the level of freedom that you have. It is considered humane to put a suffering animal out of its misery, correct? From our perspective, the same principle applies to humans. Unfortunately, some beings experience heavier restrictions than humanity does, greater suffering, and greater limitations. We understand that this information might not necessarily uplift your spirits. We are simply comparing your reality with others and assuring you that your world is not the worst of its kind. We are hopeful that this information will inspire at least a hint of gratitude in your hearts. Be grateful that you can laugh, that you can love, that you can at least have hope for a better day because there are some extraterrestrial beings who cannot. They cannot even conceive of joy or happiness. They do not even know that these things exist. This is why we encourage you humans to have gratitude.

Fantasies are in interesting subject. Romantic fantasies, for example, are a type of fantasy that is very common on your world. Did you know that every single fantasy you ever had will be satisfied in some place and time? There is no such thing as a question without an answer, and as such, there is no such thing as desire without satisfaction. The difference between your desires and fantasies in the physical plane versus the spirit plane is that there is a great deal of time lag. In the spirit plane, your will and desires are met instantly. In physicality, however, due to the process of time, it can take up to millions of years before you get what you want. This is why Creation is so vast. The infinity of desires that The Creator has (that you have) literally takes an infinity of space, time, and realities to fulfill.

Whether your fantasies are positive or negative, selfish or selfless, they will all be experienced and satisfied in some fashion or another. From our perspective, you are fulfilling someone else's fantasy right now as we speak. The majority of humanity has agreed to be temporarily suppressed, or enslaved, and we wish to emphasize *temporarily* because it is important for you to understand that if you were truly as powerless as you sometimes think you are, you would have no chance for freedom at all. Your will for freedom is being honored by Creation, just as any other will or desire in existence. However, there is a time lag to manifestation in physicality.

Once upon a time, there were beings who dreamed of amassing great power, who yearned to be worshiped and feared. You are fulfilling their fantasy by participating in this Earth reality right now. That which you call the shadow government or global elites, beings of great status and power on your planet, were once average folk in other realities who dreamed of being powerful. They wanted the experience of superiority, of god-like status over all others within their reality. And so, their will is now being met, their fantasy is being fulfilled, and it is the love that you had for these beings that allows that to be so. They are not forcing you to submit, as it appears from your physical perspective. From the spiritual perspective, you are magnifying their light by willingly diminishing your own. This is a gift you are giving them, and it is a gift that has been given to you in past lives by others as well.

One cannot experience oneself as powerful or superior unless her or she interacts with beings who are inferior by comparison. You diminish your power, your intelligence, your strength, your freedom, etc., so that someone else can feel superior compared to you. You are gifting them the experience of power, and when the time comes, they will gift you in return (if they haven't already). The experience of power and superiority is sought by many souls throughout the multiverse, and out of love and playfulness, we willingly grant each other this experience; we take turns in playing the superior role. Though this concept may be difficult for some of you to understand, we are merely sharing our objective point of view.

This may appear impossible to you. "I would never do such a thing," you may think, and yes, you as the current role or identity you are donning would not. However, you are everything in existence. The Creator is you, and you are The Creator. There is only One being is all of Creation, and it is the desire of The One to experience every concept that exists within its infinite imagination. For example, did you know there is a zombie apocalypse taking place on a parallel version of Earth right now as we speak? The Pleiadian Alliance has assisted many worlds that have undergone global pandemics. We are currently assisting eleven other worlds, including yours. One of them, in the Antares star system, is facing potential extinction due to a viral disease that causes skin decomposition, violent irritability, and compelling carnivorism.

Does this concept sound familiar? The point we are making is that every concept, every imaging that has crossed the human mind is in fact a tangible reality that is being played out somewhere within the infinite multiverse. Many of your fictional concepts are actually real-life events happening elsewhere within parallel versions of your own planet. The problem, our problem, is that negativity is overwhelming the universe and we do not wish to live in a negative-status universe any longer.

Some of you may wonder why we simply do not leave the universe and migrate to a different one. We cannot do this for many reasons. First of all, we have sympathy with those that would be left behind, our loved ones. We simply couldn't take the trillions of souls within the universe with us. Not all souls would want to leave to begin with. Even if we informed each and every soul about a coming universal apocalypse, there are many "die hard" residents that would be too stubborn to listen. Second of all, evacuating the universe is not so simple. There are malevolent guardians that prevent souls from leaving the universe. Some of your conspiracy circles refer to Earth as a "prison planet," a planet where souls are trapped inside the planetary matrix and are prevented from leaving. Well, in some regards, the entire universe can be considered one cosmic prison as well.

Propagating a doomsday scenario is not our intention. Trust us, humans, we Pleiadians are not pessimists. If a soul truly desired to evacuate from this universe, it could. There are many souls who come and go in and out of the universe. As people on your planet say – if there's a will, there's a way. This knowing is prevalent throughout the Pleiades as well. We share many common beliefs with you. The problem is that we shouldn't have to worry about leaving or evacuating. We should not have to live with the constant fear of war or apocalyptic end times, which is why it is important that we heal the universe, beginning especially with the nexus points.

We remind you that progress is being made. The probabilities are in our favor. During every birth/death cycle of the universe, after every big bang that occurs, the universe undergoes many different phases and cycles. Some of these cycles are dark or negative, others are light and positive. Each birth/death cycle comes with at least one dark age that lasts for billions of years. However, light ages or golden ages typically last much longer. Just as your Earth and humanity undergoes many rises and falls, so too does the universe. The general themes of these cycles repeat over and over but the specifics are always different. However, you and the rest of the universe are at an unprecedented crossroads. The next path we are about to take will determine our fate into a long-lasting heaven or hell.

On a subconscious level, our collective consciousness speaks with yours, and we are proud of the agreements you have made, for we need your cooperation. You have agreed to transmute yourselves, to ascend and return to harmonious balance among yourselves. The Crown of the Cosmos has chosen the path of light. And this excites us very much.

Polar Forces of Creation

The messages I received in this chapter are about good and evil. I asked Deltavash why anyone would choose to live in a reality that is filled with so much pain. I keep hearing from spiritual teachers that we are constantly creating our own reality, no matter how unpleasant it may be. I find this hard to believe considering I've had some dark moments that I'm sure I never would have chosen for myself. Her response was a rather lengthy yet interesting one.

Deltavash: Creation always finds balance. From your individual point of view, it may appear as if reality is a ladder with some beings having grand experiences at the top and others having miserable experiences at the bottom. This is the nature of existence at any given moment. However, along the process of time, Creation always brings equality and balance. Understand that no matter the intensity of pain, no matter how unpleasant the situation may be, there is divine purpose within all things.

Every soul in Creation naturally gravitates to its most essential state – the neutral state. The Creator is not biased to good or evil. The Creator, the source of all things, is fundamentally neutral, and thus, so are we. If we decide to polarize and experience ourselves as good or evil, we will always make our way back to the neutral state. That is a guarantee. In order to achieve this, our energy field must be in balance.

You may despise someone here in physical reality, yet at the spirit level, there is only love. Therefore, if you caused someone pain in one life, when you return to the spirit level, you will naturally seek to establish balance. Even the most sadistic of souls on your planet will experience remorse when they return to spirit consciousness. Out of love and friendship, you put yourself through pain to allow balance between yourself and those you have harmed, and vice versa. This is called karma. It is never about punishment. Karma is always about balance and love; it is about having an equal share of experiences. The Creator loves all beings equally, and at the divine level of spirit, so do you.

Suffering or sacrifice can be a gift you decide to give. This understand this information may be difficult for some of you to digest, but the truth is, we sometimes sacrifice ourselves for the benefit of others. At the spirit level, you agree to diminish your light in order to allow someone else's light to shine brighter.

Imagine a room filled with candles. If all the candles are shining equally, then none of them get to stand out. Yet if all but one of them diminish their brightness, then the one left shining will experience itself as brighter and higher candle than the rest.

This exalting experience is highly desirable among souls throughout the multiverse. Out of love, souls throughout Creation willing allow each other to outshine one another, even though it appears to be nonconsensual from your physical point of view. The majority of you humans have sacrificed yourselves many times out of love for others, and many of your loved ones have done the same for you. We all take turns in glorifying one another and allowing each other the opportunity to feel bigger and brighter than the rest.

Allow us to be frank with you – why does evil exist, you ask? Because it's fun to be evil. Yes, it's fun to have friends to share life and joys with, but it can also be fun to have enemies to fight and win victorious battles against. What you call "fun" is the point of existence. The goal of every soul is identical; every soul throughout Creation wants to be happy. However, there are many ways to achieve happiness (pleasure). It is not always achieved in a sharing manner; it can be achieved through acts of selfishness and greed as well, by exalting yourself at someone else's expense.

Positive realities are based on mutual pleasure for everyone involved; one for all. Negative realities are based on pleasure only for the winner or superior; all for one. This is true in your reality, yes? You have collectively created a reality in which only one percent of the population is afforded abundance of power and freedom while the majority is left in poverty and all manner of ruins.

In truth, all realities are based on equality because Creation always finds balance. Every reality in existence is co-created by spirits in mutual agreement to join together and play a game, to interact with each other within the parameters and themes of a particular setting. When a group of souls decide to play in a negative reality, a competitive reality, they always take turns in being the winner or "top dog" so that everyone can have a fair chance at enjoyment. You would not enter into a negative reality without a fair chance at experience the pleasurable side of it. This is the true meaning of karma. Simply put, when a soul chooses to harm another, it automatically chooses to be harmed in return, for balance. This decision of course is made at the spirit level.

We wish to further discuss the concept of evil. From our perspective, all of you contain the potential for evil inside you. Have you ever wished to be a celebrity? Or how about an athletic champion? Did you ever fantasize about being wealthy, famous, powerful, or superior to other people in any way? The desire to put yourself above others is the root of all evil. This desire stems from the ego. Ego-driven entities, or evil people as you call them, are not interested in fair share and equality; they are only interested in superiority.

Evil is a form of consciousness. It is a type of mentality that believes itself to be superior. The root of all evil is the ego, the aspect from which our sense of self-love and self-worth stem from. When you encounter beings you refer to as "evil," you are encountering that which is highly focused and navigating reality from an ego-based point of view. Their sense of self-worth is so high that they believe themselves to be deserving of the best experiences. One cannot feel superior if others are having an equal-to or greater-than experience. Therefore, the objective that evil beings tend to commonly have is to lower the quality of experiences held by others. It is for this reason that they are notorious for bringing pain, misery and destruction. Rather than uplifting the light within others, they wish to diminish it; to shroud everyone in darkness so that they can feel like the shining candle in a dark room. And as much as some of you may refuse to believe it, dear friends, negative realities have granted you some of the most exhilarating experiences.

Evil exists because it's fun to be evil. Negative realities would not exist otherwise. Celebrities, champions, the rich and powerful would not exist in your reality if they didn't have inferior people to compare themselves to. And since most of you have desired to feel better or superior to other beings at some point in your lives, you have co-created and perpetuated a reality in which the contrast of superior and inferior life experiences exist. How can you achieve a superior experience if you do not have someone lower and less fortunate in your reality to compare yourself to? You may not wish to harm someone in your pursuit of a celebrity or winning status, but regardless of the degree of superiority you seek, it is that self-serving portion of you from which all evil stems.

One thing we wish to point out, dear friends, is that none of you are inherently better than anyone else. It may appear as if you are smarter than someone because you can easily beat them at games or calculate equations much quicker, or that you are more lovable because you have a more attractive body, or that you are luckier because you were born into wealth. The truth is, all of us can create the illusion of superiority. Those that are beneath you in this lifetime can easily become your superiors in the next. For example, you may think that you are an inherently smart person, yet try incarnating into a body with poor genes that render the brain sluggish and slow. How smart would you consider yourself then? All things are relative; strong is relative to the weak, fast is relative to the slow, cruel is relative to the kind, etc. You may think that the identity you currently don is your one and only true self, but allow us to remind you – your imagination is infinite, and just as you can create a pleasant dream in one night, you can just as easily create a petrifying nightmare the very next. You can focus your consciousness in ever-changing ways. Consider that for a moment.

Angels and Demons

Allow us to clarify some misunderstandings about the heart chakra and the ego chakra. Your spiritual communities believe that the heart chakra is the key to enlightenment. They put the heart chakra on a pedestal while rejecting the ego chakra as bad or wrong. We strongly disagree with this belief system. The ego is the aspect of you that feels deserving, worthy, and entitled to anything it desires. When you operate out of balance, with too much heart and neglect of the ego, you can become too humble, too low in self-esteem and feeling undeserving of your desires.

People on your planet who operate with too much heart often find themselves exploited by others. They become unable to refuse service to others and will often put the needs of others before their own, even if they feel exhausted and run down. We do not see this as a healthy or positive mindset. When you are in balance with both your heart and ego aspects, you can then play on an equal basis with other beings, giving and receiving service equally. This is the key to mutual pleasure and the basis for spiritual societies. This is the direction we see you moving in, and your year of 2017 will highlight the worldwide beginnings of this movement.

Ultimately, there are only two sensations that exist in Creation: pleasure and pain. Love is the emotion that follows pleasure. Fear is the emotion that follows pain. These two sensations are respectively associated with the male and female aspects of Creation. The heart chakra wants to be loved, the ego chakra wants to be feared. These are the polar forces of Creation.

An angel, by our definition, is a heart-centered being, one driven to nurture, heal and elate others, one who enjoys being a source of beauty and pleasure in order to receive love and affection in return. Women physiologically embody the heart. This is partly why women grow breasts. The heart chakra is located in the chest area; a bigger chest physiologically symbolizes a bigger heart. Femininity is stereotypically associated with beauty and love. Female bodies are designed with the creative ability to birth, nurse, and raise life. In general, women excel at romance, at kindness, at bringing and uplifting life; service-to-others.

A demon, by our definition, is an ego-centered individual, one who desires power and status over others, who uses pain in order to elicit fear and submission and to lower the state of others in order to exalt its own by contrast. When you shut down the heart chakra and fully concentrate your consciousness on the ego, you effectively become a demon. Males physiologically represent the ego. This is partly why males have bigger genitals. The ego chakra is located in the genital region; a bigger genitelia symbolizes a bigger ego. It is for this reason that men are designed with greater physical strength, stature and power. In general, men excel at war and destruction, aggression and domination; service to self.

You can see the contrast in these polarities - the angel or female is the creator of life, the demon or male is the destroyer. These definitions apply to men and women only in extreme cases of polarization. We acknowledge that most men on your planet are not demonic, and most women are not exactly angelic. Extreme polarization does not occur in most realities. Societies with the utmost health are ones that are in balance with their male and female aspects, where all individuals are equally empowered with masculine strength and equally nurtured with feminine love.

We do not suggest putting feminine energy on a pedestal, dear friends. The desires of the heart chakra can be generous and noble, yet you can observe on your planet alone that women are often the gender riddled with the greatest amount of self-love issues. Women often find themselves dependent on others for love, validation, and assurance. They sometimes sacrifice their health, comfort, and truth in order to feel accepted. When you neglect your ego (your male chakra), you may find yourself dependent and sometimes subservient, bending to the will of others in exchange for love or survival. We advise you to not neglect or devalue your ego. In moderation, the ego is your source of dignity and self-empowerment. There is equal value and divinity in both the feminine and masculine aspects of Creation.

The heart chakra is the key to world peace, yet it can be unpredictable. Empathy is a double-edged sword. When your heart is open to someone, you assimilate their feelings; you feel what they feel. You can achieve a variety of experiences vicariously through other people via the heart chakra. You do this when you watch a movie and experience highs and lows of emotions vicariously through the characters on screen. There are some women who have achieved great satisfaction through the heinous actions committed by their partners. Believe it or not, you can actually use the heart chakra to nurture the dark nature of certain people and derive pleasure from the nefarious crimes they commit. Just as a father can live vicariously through the athletic victories of his son, so too can seemingly sane and innocent people live vicariously through dark and sadistic individuals. What you use your heart chakra to connect with is up to you.

Balance is not about androgyny. We are not suggesting that a man must surrender his masculinity or that a woman must surrender her femininity. Each of you are a composite of three different aspects: a mind, a body, and a soul. Each one of these aspects has its own gender, so to speak. From our perspective, you each have a mental gender, a physical gender, and an emotional gender. Some humans on your planet may have a physical gender that is male, yet they may undoubtedly have a mental identity that is female, yes? One can achieve a balanced emotional/spiritual aspect without compromising their mental or physical gender.

Your mental gender, or gender identity, is not affected by being in balance. The aspect that must come into balance is the soul, the spiritual, emotional gender. When your emotional aspect is in balance, you are not aggressive and domineering of others, nor are you passive and submissive to others; you are assertive; you get what you want without harming others or allowing others to harm you. This is the key to humanity's salvation and ascension.

To be assertive is to be in balance. You can be assertive and still have a masculine or feminine personality. When humanity dons an assertive mentality, you will not be easily controlled by others. To us, being an aggressive person is just as negative as being a passive one. This is why aggressive and passive beings tend to meet – winners always find losers, masters always find slaves. Your world is heavily submersed in these scenarios. If you wish to emancipate yourselves from these negative interactions, you must become assertive. The more that each of you individually become assertive and establish positive relationships based on mutual respect with all others, the sooner you will dismantle the hierarchical superior/inferior structure of your society and establish a society that is based on harmonious equality instead.

Male energy is aggressive. When a world is overflowing with male energy, this typically creates a world driven by competition; wars thrive endlessly until there is only one man standing or until the world is completely destroyed. When ego-based individuals interact with each other, they typically tend to compete for power and domination of all goods and resources. Conversely, female energy is passive, and when a planet is overflowing with this energy, it often becomes cooperative and peaceful; there is little to no competition and the world is driven by the sharing of goods and resources. However, when too much passive energy is flowing, reality can easily become uneventful. Passive civilizations are also more prone to invasion and conquest by others.

Believe it or not, most souls do not stay in utopian realities for long. They easily get bored. Most souls throughout Creation prefer some degree of drama and challenge to spice up their existence. Having problems to solve can be stimulating and fun.

Therefore, a healthy balance of male and female energy is most often preferred. This is why the fifth dimension is so popular. We will further discuss the fifth dimension later on.

While most souls prefer to have a friend instead of an enemy, there are countless souls who genuinely prefer the enemy experience – the battle, the action, the victory! Having an enemy can be very exciting in some cases. This is why war and conflict have existed alongside peace and friendship from the very beginning of Creation. This is also why it is important not to judge the dark side. There is not a single human on Earth who has not experienced dark urges to some degree.

Most of you, by the time you are of adults, have experienced anger, greed, and envy to some extent. You all contain the potential for evil and acts of greed within you, so we encourage you to not judge the dark side since it is merely another aspect of yourself. Evil beings are simply people who are sensitive to negative emotions and are focusing their consciousness on the self-serving ego. We encourage you to be objective, not biased. Remember that having a bad enemy, in some cases, can be just as fun as having a good friend. While most souls prefer interactions that are based on equality, there are others who genuinely prefer superiority. This is part of Creation's infinite diversity.

Most of you have been both male and female, good and evil in past lives. You have been a number of many different things. The soul is infinitely versatile, unlimited in flexibility. You can think of your soul as a body of air. If you were to go to Antarctica, you would experience yourself as cold air, if you were to go to the Sahara, you would experience yourself as hot air. You can become air that is high pressure, low pressure, dry, humid, polluted or rainforest fresh – anything you wish! Your consciousness can attune itself to any experience you can imagine.

It might interest you to know that within The Pleiadian Alliance there are beings who can change their gender identity at will. You, as humans, must wait entire lifetimes to switch between being male or female. There are some of us on other worlds and dimensions who can literally be male in one second and become wholly female the next. Masculine expressions are sometimes more suitable in certain situations; feminine expressions are sometimes more suitable in other situations. According to what situation is at hand and how we wish to react, we can alternate between masculine and feminine expressions. In much higher dimensions, it is even common for beings to alternate their physical form between male and female in the blink of an eye. While you humans wait whole lifetimes for your chance to experience yourself as the opposite gender, some beings regularly change their gender from moment to moment, alternating thousands of times within a single incarnation. They are not bound exclusively to one side of polarity; they are free to switch fluidly back and forth. A long time from now, in the distant future, humanity will gain this ability.

Most of you believe that male energy is responsible for all the negativity existing on your planet. We do not agree with this. From our perspective, female energy is equally responsible. The situation of Earth is one of disempowerment. Your governments are like an abusive husband while the general population is a passive, submissive wife. Are the majority of people on your planet rebellious? Do they demand equality and fair share between themselves and ruling powers? From our point of view, there is an excess amount of passive, female energy among your population. Most of you are highly complacent and compliant, passively giving away your power to government officials and allowing others to control your lives. You are passengers in a vehicle driven by madmen.

There is a saying that evil thrives when good people do nothing, yes? The passive or female energy is greatly part of what perpetuates this problem. This is what allows you to be easily subjugated by malevolent beings. In order to have a society where goods and resources are abundant for all, you must first feel worthy of it. You must desist from complacent, submissive behavior to authority figures and establish relationships based on mutual respect and mutual pleasure. Once humanity becomes collectively assertive, genuinely dignified and demanding of equality from leaders in a non-aggressive, non-violent manner, this is when you will experience redistribution of power on your world and the true beginnings of a new golden age.

PLEIADIAN PROPHECIES

This chapter is my collection of predictions shared with me by my guide. I have been fascinated with the future since I was a teenager. I remember there was so much talk about the year 2012, the end of the Mayan calendar being a time of significant change for humanity, and I remember how disappointed I was when nothing major happened on that date. We are years passed 2012 and yet there is still an overwhelming amount of war, poverty, disease and suffering in the world. I asked my guide about the future of our world, how long it will take for us to change our reality for the better, and the messages I received were so interesting and excited, they compelled me to write this book.

Deltavash: Prophecy is a mysterious craft that is poorly understood or defined on your world. Since the majority of predictions made by your psychics do not come true, many people are skeptical about prophecy and its reliability. From our perspective, prophecy is only reliable for the prediction of general outcomes; it is not reliable for the prediction of specific outcomes.   One analogy is your weather forecasts – you can accurately predict the arrival of winter, but can you predict the exact days of rain, snow, or sunshine? In the same way, we cannot predict the details of your journey, for you are constantly writing and re-writing the story as you go along, but we can predict the general flows of energy, the start and end of time cycles, the overall direction you are headed, what we foresee on the horizon for the time being. All roads lead to Rome – you will reach your destination one way or another, and your destination, dear friends, is one of sheer paradise.

The Pleiadian Alliance is honored to share some predictive insight with you. During the time of Atlantis, which reigned between 35 thousand and 15 thousand years ago in your history, humans were fully psychic, multidimensional beings who could view the outcomes of their actions beforehand. You were literally able to read probable futures based on your actions in the present moment. It was like previewing the events played out throughout your day before actually living it, and you could consciously choose which version of the future you preferred to experience. This ability is still carried within you. However, it has been largely shut down on the genetic level. But not to worry, dear friends, the time is approaching when these genetic codes will reactivate and awaken your innate psychic abilities once again. In the meantime, it is our pleasure to share what we can foresee coming to your world.

The concept of a timeline is relevant only in linear time. Because of the highly focused nature of your consciousness, it appears as if there is only reality that you are moving through at any given time. Here in fourth density, where we reside, time is also mostly linear. However, we are able to perceive time from a multidimensional point of view to some extent.

When you reach a multidimensional, spirit-level view of reality, it transcends your perspective of linear time. Think of linear time as a trail on a road map. Picture a road map in your mind for a moment. Let us use a map of the United States as an example – imagine having a magnifying glass in your hand that you are using to view a map. Your consciousness, your mind, is the magnifying glass. When you bring the magnifying glass down and focus it entirely on the city of Los Angeles on the west coast, you must move the magnifying glass across the map in order to reach New York City on the east coast. You thus create a line on this map, or a "timeline" to shift from the west coast reality to the east coast. When you reach New York, you can thus say, "I had a past life in Los Angeles." However, if you were to raise the magnifying glass (your consciousness) high enough to view the entire map, you would then be able to see Los Angeles and New York City at the same time. You would thus experience yourself being in both places at once! This is how consciousness works; you can focus your mind down to the level of a single reality, a single place and time, or you can raise your mind up to a higher level to see the bigger picture, multiple realities existing concurrently.

Being that you are third density beings with limited foresight, we will attempt to illustrate what your probable future looks like as best we can. Again, we share a sense of linear time here in fourth density as well, so we empathize with your curiosity about the future very much. Before we begin laying out a list of probable futures for you, we wish to briefly discuss the concept of destiny and fate.

If you were to look at the energetic makeup behind any reality, you would see it as a multidimensional, geometric figure. The energetic foundation behind every reality is an energetic blueprint or pattern that lays out the path or themes for each reality. In a sense, every reality is like a snowflake. As you know on your world, every snowflake is unique, and just as every snowflake has distinctive patterns with their own shapes and cycles, so too does the very reality you exist in.

The Earth reality has gone through numerous cycles of ascension and descension. Your Hindu philosophy has the general understanding of these cycles, called Yugas. Essentially, your world shifts between light ages and dark ages repeatedly. Light ages, or golden ages, last for approximately 20 thousand years on your world. In these ages, humanity experiences profound beauty, spirituality, social equality and peace. Knowledge is power, and thus, golden ages are a time of enlightenment where all participants are self-empowered with divine wisdom. This is an age of love and unity where the heart chakra connects all living beings. Atlantis was the most recent golden age on Earth.

Following the heart-chakra theme of the golden age is first age of descension which we will call the post-golden age. During this phase, which lasts approximately 15 thousand years, humanity begins to shift away from spirituality and gains an increasing interest in materialism. Although spirituality is still widespread, the ego chakra begins to amplify during this age and people become somewhat greedy. The Atlanteans experienced this age as a time of self-indulgence, using technology for physical pleasure and the acquisition of luxurious jewelry, among other things. They did not experience war or slavery among themselves, but they did experiment with servitude similar to the maids and waiters you have on your world. Their society shifted away from social equality and into a relatively benign hierarchical structure during this age.

After the post-golden age comes the pre-dark age. Pre-dark ages last for approximately 10 thousand years. They are a time where ignorance and materialism begin to outweigh spirituality, and societies become either patriarchal or matriarchal in a hierarchical structure that introduces moderate levels of slavery and war. In your history, this phase began after the Atlanteans destroyed much of their world via a technological experiment that resulted in a cataclysmic disaster. The remains of Atlantis in your Atlantic Ocean were later submerged by massive flooding. All Atlantean artifacts, knowledge, and records were lost. As a side note, one common belief throughout the Pleiades, dear friends, is that whenever something is lost, it is always meant to be found.

Following the pre-dark age is the full-fledge demonic period known as the dark age, an age where materialistic greed takes precedence, where the ego chakra possesses humanity and spirituality is forgotten. Dark ages last for approximately 5 thousand years and are a time of pervasive disempowerment and competition. The Earth becomes shrouded in darkness as human life becomes focused on survival, famine, disease, war, brutal hierarchy, hate and fear. As an age of ignorance where spiritual truth is scarce and withdrawn, this is an age where humanity experiences enslavement by its own tyrannical authority figures.

After dark ages come to an end, it takes approximately 400 years for humanity to reconnect with itself, regain its wisdom, and establish a new golden age. These cycles, or Yugas, have occurred in your linear history at least three times, according to our data. You are now approaching the end of the third and final dark age on your timeline.

The good news is that you will not have to wait 400 years to establish a new golden age. This third and final dark age will officially end between the fall equinox of 2016 and the winter solstice of 2017. However, instead of taking 400 years to reach the light at the end of the tunnel, this time around, it will only take about 10 years! As we read the energetics of your world, the geometric path you are moving through, we see that the new golden age will be established no later than 2027!

General Forecast

The first thing we wish to address in regards to your future is the collective energy of your world. Currently, your collective energy is predominantly negative. Because of this, those who are in alignment with this flow of energy are generally the ones who have the best of luck. If you are a negative being in a negative reality, then you are going with the flow. Because of this, things tend to work out for you. However, if you are a positive being existing in a negative reality, then you are likely to experience a great degree of resistance, friction, frustration, and general bad luck because you are going against the flow of your reality. This is often why many of you ask the question, "why do bad things happen to good people?"

The exciting news about your near future is that the table is about to turn – your world will become predominantly positive beginning in or around the year 2017. That means that if you are a being who is of positive orientation (and if you are reading this book, you most likely are), the collective energy will begin to support you more and more as it adjusts and gets in alignment with your frequency. This means that good people on your world will experience an increase in good luck very soon! Those who are negative in nature will begin to experience increasing amounts of friction and frustration as the collective energy no longer supports them. There is a saying throughout the Pleiades that we wish to share with you here – he who goes with the flow is always the luckiest man standing. Remember this.

Your planet is under global depression right now. Meaning, the majority of humanity is experiencing high amounts of stress and fear, effectively creating an atmosphere that accommodates negative entities. This global depression is caused primarily by your economic system, a system designed to empower a minority of people on your planet while leaving the greater majority in ruins. Because of this global depression, you are a frequency match for low-frequency entities. This is why your planet is infested with malevolent visitors. When you lower your vibration, you become a frequency match for low-frequency entities.

Essentially, by lowering your frequency, you are meeting low-frequency beings eye-to-eye; you bring yourself down to their level and can thus perceive and interact with them directly. If you wish to meet positive extraterrestrials or angelic beings eye-to-eye, you must elevate your frequency to match their level. It is very much like lowering yourself into the deep blue sea where you meet the sharks. If you wish to interact with the soaring seagulls instead, you must raise your state of being above the waters and into the clouds. Wherever you place yourself on the vibrational ladder, those are the beings you will encounter.

We sense profound economic changes coming soon to your world, and we are excited to see the positive wonders that will ensue from this. By the winter solstice of 2017, significant economic changes will occur. This will raise the collective vibration of humanity considerably, the demonic infestation of Earth will begin to die off, and you will notice a radical change of luck in your daily lives. Good luck and positive synchronicities will become more and more prevalent throughout your lives from that point forward.

Beginning 2017, new changes to the economy will continue to escalate. Eventually, no later than 2027, there will be no more poverty or starvation on your planet. Humanity will establish free energy and economic fairness for all. This will remove the demon infestation completely and allow for the angels, your spirit guides, and extraterrestrial friends to step through the energetic veil and greet you all face-to-face.

The Political System

Your political and economic systems originate from the Orion star system. Millions of years ago, civilizations within the Orion system experienced an extreme degree of oppression. The tyranny that currently exists on your planet is only a miniature replica of what was established in the ancient Orion system. The beings there were heavily controlled under strict regulations and unrealistic expectations. If you can imagine the anxiety most of you experience when a police officer appears driving behind you, this type of scenario was common throughout every aspect of the Orion society, only far worse. Beings were expected to meet regulations with impeccable, computer-perfect flawlessness. There was no tolerance for even the slightest error, and unimaginably horrific consequences for what would equate on your world to a mere misdemeanor.

Though there is great horror that exists in your reality, particularly at the underground level, the Orion system was masterly with its tyrannical use of advanced technology to create and maintain an atmosphere of penetrating fear that empowered the sadistic, vampiric rulers of that unspeakable time. In a general overview, the degree of oppression and suffering that existed in the ancient Orion system was approximately 10 thousand times more intense than any pain experienced on Earth. The vast majority of souls incarnated into your Earth reality currently have karmic ties with each other that were established in the ancient Orion system. It has literally taken millions of years for you to restore balance and release those grudges, but you are rapidly approaching the finish line of releasing those ties.

The years 2017 and 2018 will see a reduction in the authoritative power of government officials. There will be great political scandals and government exposure between 2016 and 2019. It is your destiny to gain awareness. Part of that awareness has to do with the truth about your authority figures. While many believe that they serve to protect you, the time will come when their true colors are revealed. The corrupt nature of your self-serving governments must be exposed before a new political system can emerge.

Gradually, between the years of 2017 and 2022, humanity will begin to establish social and political systems that are based on true democracy. In other words, the voice of the people will be heard and the heart of the people will be served. What do you desire? Do you want more wars? Do you want more taxes? Do you want free markets? What do you think should be legal? What should be illegal?

Instead of creating and enforcing the laws, government workers will serve as mediators or facilitators between the law and the democratic demands of the general public. An end to ruling with an iron fist will emerge no later than 2022 in the United States, and no later than 2030 for all other nations. A true democracy will emerge, where laws and decisions are made and based on the majority rule of the people. Greed will no longer be the deciding factor of civil and political outcomes. You are shifting from a society that has an all-for-one mentality into a society that is geared towards one-for-all. The activated heart chakra of humanity will be instrumental in facilitating this new way of thinking.

One very special change coming to the political system is power to individual workers. Currently, the majority of you are at the mercy of your employers, your boss. You strive to appease your leaders, to impress them so that you keep your job, yet how often do bosses do the same for their employees? In most cases, your superiors can easily evade penalties without fear of persecution. We, The Pleiadian Alliance, do not fear our leaders. There is mutual respect between all workers within our organization. There have been cases where some of our leaders get "fired" by the group of beings they were assigned to lead. In your history, many revolts have occurred, oppressive kings have been dethroned and tyrannical leaders have been overthrown. We see more of this happening on your world but on a smaller scale, in your workforce. Disrespect and abusive behavior by your leaders will simply not be tolerated by the awakened human population. Expect a lot more workers speaking up and uniting against tyrannical leaders on a national scale, as well as the corporate and small business scale.

We gladly wish to mention that prison systems will see a significant decline in the number of inmates. With economic freedom reaching new heights with each passing year after 2017, the urge to steal or lash out of poverty-induced frustration will become less and less common. We perceive an approximation of 25% drop in inmate count around 2020, a 60% drop around 2025, a 90% drop by 2035, and a 100% by 2040. There will still be misdemeanors and other minor cases of immature, impulsive behavior, but serious crimes will no longer apply to your reality by 2050 as we now perceive it.

With regards to world government, there is a high probability that a unified one-world government will emerge within this century. It will begin with an increasing number of united nations. Eventually, your entire world will unify as one cooperative family. The diversity of races and cultures on your planet calls for personalized governments to last for some time; that which works for one culture may not be so favorable to another. However, you will eventually recognize that you are all fundamentally alike. Every human has the same basic desires for social acceptance, creative expression, etc. In time, a planetary culture will emerge that encourages all individuals to do whatever makes them happy so long as they do not bring harm to others. The "no harm, no foul" mentality is prevalent throughout the Pleiades. The majority of our societies live according to policies and code of conduct that allows freedom of expression for all beings so long as none are harmed. This will become the umbrella mindset that will begin to flourish on your world by 2020 and will be the basis for the unified planetary culture that will emerge by 2040. We are very excited to see this probable future unfold.

The Economy

Most of you believe that money is the biggest problem on your world. From our perspective, this is incorrect. The biggest problem is actually your genetic programming. Money, and the hierarchical societies that it creates, is only a byproduct. The reason a brutal economic hierarchy exists is because it resonates with your genetic programming. You are a species that is responsive and reactive to certain ideas in very specific ways. You are a species that does not question authority. You are complacent, fearful, and submissive. These genetic traits are the engine that have kept your corrupt economic system running for so long. We assure you, a new economic system will emerge as soon as the old one no longer resonates with the general population.

The human genome is in dire need of activation. You cannot create a new golden age with the current programming you carry. It is very much like expecting a computer to perform a feat that it is simply not built to perform. You cannot expect a pocket calculator to perform the various tasks of a modern personal computer, nor can you expect the loving friendliness of a dog from something as antisocial as a crocodile; they are simply not built for it. In the same way, you are not built for a golden age; you are currently built for a dark age. As a result of the genetic codes that block your higher chakras, you navigate this reality concerned primarily with physical survival. The multidimensional nature of your existence is unbeknownst to most of you. Without awareness of your true identity and inner power, you are susceptible to deception and manipulation. This, however, is changing.

Your genetic makeup is reactivating. Energies from the galactic core, as well as the photon belt from the Pleiadian star of Alcyone, are bombarding the Earth, causing electromagnetic stimulation that is toggling your genetic switches from off to on. This is the ascension process that your spiritual community is raving about. Not before long, all that once seemed logical and sensible to you will suddenly appear illogical, insane, and barbaric – your economic system in particular. If you want a golden age, you must allow your DNA to blossom. Do not resist this process. We encourage you to relax your mind and open your heart. The more each of you go with the flow and embrace the coming changes without resistance, the sooner this ascension process can complete.

As we scan your timeline, the first major change we see coming to your economy is the redistribution of wealth. This is vital to your ascension. Currently, your economy has an all-for-one structure; those at the top receive the highest amount of compensation (regardless of their work or time input) while the majority of people receive poverty wages. This is certainly not suitable for a golden age. By the end of 2017, you will start to experience the redistribution of wealth on your world.

The practice of distributing poverty wages is a cold and deliberate one. Not only will poverty wages disappear across the globe around 2020, but working hours will see a significant decline as well. Before these changes can emerge, humanity must turn away from complacency. You must initiate a movement towards economic equality by bridging the gap between rich and poor. All workers deserve fair compensation, not just those on top of the pyramid. We are very excited to see this particular prediction unfold, and believe us when we say, there will be tremendous opposition by those in power against this movement, but it will unfold despite their wishes anyway.

Many conspiracy theorists foretell of a global economic collapse. From our perspective, there is 50% probability of this occurring. If a global economic collapse occurs, it will incite the general public to vocalize disapproval of current economic systems in masses. Public outrage and protests may be widespread. On the other hand, you will make economic adjustments that steer society towards equality either way. You have the option of attaining a more egalitarian economy the fast way, through a traumatic economic collapse that triggers immediate action, or the slow way, through gradual changes that allow people time to adjust. Whichever path you collectively choose to take, we are confident that global economic stability and equality will be achieved between 2024 and 2028.

Economic relief equates to global relief (relief of the global depression). You need this, and we encourage you to actively participate in any campaign that promotes living wages for all citizens. There will still be leaders and followers in the golden age. Not everyone wants to take charge or have the most responsibility. However, on Alpha Earth, each individual will be allowed whatever position is most comfortable for them without judgment or penalties.

If you prefer to have the least authoritative position in a work group, that will be afforded to you without relegation to poverty, ridicule or shame. Every aspect of a company is required to make the whole successful. Therefore, by 2027, the gap between rich and poor will be virtually nonexistent.

By the winter solstice of 2017, we sense the beginnings of a new economic system. There will be much debt relief, minimum wage increase, and new laws that enforce unprecedented tax hikes on wealthy citizens. No later than 2020, a new wave of economic alterations will emerge. This will include a significant decrease in the possible accumulation of individual wealth. Billionaires will become extinct by 2024 and millionaires will find it increasingly difficult to maintain their multi-million-dollar income. By your year of 2027, the rich and powerful will cease to exist. This is an indication that your genetic material will be vastly different by this point, providing you with a higher understanding of reality and a more assertive outlook on life.

We perceive a one-world currency emerging at some point. The highest probability highlights the year 2022 in which this process may begin. By this point, currency exchange will be largely conducted through virtual or digital means, not paper and coins. Of course this will call for an increase of jobs throughout the world. New businesses, new work centers and services will appear in third world countries at a rapid rate. Around 2035, you will succeed in establishing a one-world currency that accommodates all people worldwide. From this, a fully cooperative, unified Earth society that transcends all national borders can emerge. And it is at this time that extraterrestrial beings will begin to openly visit you in great numbers. As you establish a family-oriented mindset with each other here on Earth, it is only natural that you will attract interactions with other family-oriented beings who operate at a similar mental and emotional frequency.

Technology

The technological changes coming to your world are too many to list. We can share a general overview, however. One critical change that must occur on your planet is the integration of technology and nature. Currently, many technologies are harmful or destructive to yourselves and the environment. This of course is not suitable for a golden age. Beginning around 2018, an awakening to greater environmentally conscience innovations may arise. There were times on your planet when humans lived in harmony with nature, when Mother Earth was respected and honored. You are moving back into a more wholesome relationship with nature. Many indigenous cultures still hold high reverence for Mother Earth. Spirituality involves the establishment of love and connection with nature. As humanity becomes more spiritual, you will discover yourself gaining elevating interest in the health and well-being of the Mother Earth and all her creatures.

The industrial revolution was a time in your history when many workers were replaced by machines. We see a similar scenario emerging around 2022 – a robot revolution. This is an exciting prediction for us to share. Currently, many humans are burdened with jobs and chores that require monotonous, strenuous work. The robot revolution will bring an end to much of the hard physical labor that many people on your planet are burdened with as human workers become replaced by robot workers that are much more resilient.

We wish to share a brief side story with you. From our perspective, as The Pleiadian Alliance has observed and recorded the histories of over 100 thousand civilizations throughout the universe, we have noticed a pattern with regards to the use of robots. Generally speaking, positive societies tend to employ robots for jobs that require monotonous, strenuous work. It is considered inhumane to relegate sentient beings to the tiring pains and stresses of hard labor. Therefore, positive societies prefer to use non-sentient artificial intelligence, or robots, to perform these tasks. Negative societies, on the other hand, do not employ robots for stressful work. They instead prefer the use of fully sentient, living beings. Condemning sentient beings to lifetimes of hard labor is considered a way of enforcing hierarchy and sadistic dominance over others. This is why we are excited about sharing this prediction with you because as your world becomes more positive, you will find yourselves gradually freeing yourselves from the stresses of menial, degrading tasks that can be easily done by computerized robots instead.

The first wave of working robots that emerge on your world will be clunky and buggy compared to the more advanced editions emerging later in the 2030s. The robot revolution will be quite controversial at start, but you will quickly adapt so that living with robot helpers will be familiar and comfortable no later than 2035. Of course there will still be individuals who prefer to do their own cooking or cleaning or fixing, but in general, many of the undesirable chores and jobs that stress your bodies and minds will eventually be done by computers. A global wave of relief will undoubtedly emerge from this exciting revolution.

Again, there are many technological breakthroughs coming down your timeline. We foresee flying cars, computerized homes, free energy devices, endless advances in your entertainment industry, holographic technologies, matter and energy manipulation, not to mention the first wave of spaceship technologies and the scientific confirmation of multidimensionality coming by 2050. However, we wish to focus this topic on the robot revolution because it is the most exciting technological breakthrough on the list for us.

Free Energy

Free energy is an important subject for many of you. What the term "free energy" means to most of you is the freedom to have your basic needs met without having to work or pay for them. This would indeed be the ultimate freedom in your physical reality. What we sense coming to your world is the beginning stages of free energy around your year 2020. It will begin with certain cities, large metropolitan cities at first, granting free electricity, phone and Internet services within city limits. Quickly, this will expand into state-wide limits around the year of 2023 and eventually become nationwide in most western and European countries around 2026.

Electricity and radio-based services will be the first wave of free energy, as we see it. Eventually, you will have free purified drinking water, free food, free transportation, and free homes. All that is considered essential for basic survival will become abundant on your planet and available freely to all people no later than 2050. There are many steps you must take before you can achieve this reality, however. Many of the old systems and hierarchical mentalities must first collapse. The beginnings of free energy will be made possible as a result of changes to your taxation system. It is taxes taken from the upper class that will pay for the creation and distribution of free energy at first.

It delights us to say that by your year of 2050, replicators will be common home appliances and will provide immediate sustenance whenever needed. A replicator is a device that uses ambient energy to create almost any substance you desire. It literally restructures matter at a molecular level to form almost any product you choose. Think of it as a microwave oven that can generate delicious, nutritious, whole meals out of thin air! This will be the ultimate solution to world hunger on your planet. The Pleiadian Alliance makes frequent use of replicators, and we use them not just for food, but also for the creation of tools, clothing, furniture, even to create new replicators.

Tapping into the Earth's electromagnetic field is the key to unlimited energy on your world. You will find that the majority of machines will be powered by some source of electromagnetic energy derived from your magnetosphere, including automobiles and all other types of electronic devices. The beginnings of unlimited energy will most likely emerge around 2024 and will become a worldwide manifestation by 2040. Once unlimited energy is established, the possibilities will be endless – your progressive movement will accelerate to astronomical heights. Once you reach this point in your history, there will be nothing standing in your way. Individually and collectively, you will have your basic needs met and out of the way so that you can focus exclusively on your creative endeavors and playful, joyful celebrations with loved ones at all the time.

Extraterrestrials

Disclosure is another big topic on your world. Part of our mission is to establish open contact with you. It is generally believed that your governments are withholding valuable information about extraterrestrial intelligence. This is true, and we assure you that disclosure will occur at the appropriate timing. Currently, you are still cycling through a dark age, an age of ignorance. Knowledge of extraterrestrials that have played instrumental roles in the origin and history of your planet is not relevant information to your general population at this time, according to the themes of your current reality. What is currently relevant to your reality is mystery, wonder, and confusion. The truth about your origins and history will unfold in a timely, appropriate manner. Be patient, dear friends. You are rapidly approaching the Splitting Prism of Time. Many long-awaited revelations and adventures are on the horizon.

One of the most exciting events coming to your world is the public arrival of extraterrestrial visitors. There are already several extraterrestrial races that are interacting with you. However, most of these races are of a negative orientation. By Law of Attraction, what you pulse out vibrationally is always reflected back to you. Due to the negative status of your planet, it is very easy for negative beings to penetrate your reality. As you become more positive in nature, the tide will turn and the connection between you and positive extraterrestrials will grow stronger.

Would wish to further explain the Law of Attraction. Most of you are familiar with the concept of a Ouija board, yes? The Ouija board is an ancient tool used for divination; a link to the spirit realm. However, you might have encountered rumors or warnings about the dangers of playing the Ouija board when you are in a state of depression. By Law of Attraction, when you summon entities into your reality, if you are vibrating at a low and negative rate, then you will attract entities who vibrate at that same low frequency. This is a common phenomenon and one that is occurring at a planetary scale on your world. So long as the Earth remains globally depressed, the extraterrestrials you encounter will predominantly be of a low vibration or negative orientation.

In addition to the Law of Attraction, another interesting factor that is preventing positive extraterrestrials from interacting more directly with is the stubborn mentality of your collective consciousness. By being skeptical of extraterrestrial life and by focusing so strongly on your physical reality as if there is nothing else that exists or matters, you are basically shunning us and placing us in your blind spot. It is very much like a ghost lost and trapped inside its own bubble reality. His loved ones may be attempting to communicate with him, to reach out to him and assist him in crossing over to the other side, but he cannot see or hear them because he is so stubbornly focused on his own personal reality. This is what humanity is effectively doing –

refusing to acknowledge other realities by focusing entirely on its own. Thus, the power of your minds is blocking us from your perception.

Once you begin to open your minds about the existence of extraterrestrial life, you will then be able to interact more directly and openly with extraterrestrial beings. This begins of course in the Splitting Prism of Time, between the fall equinox of 2016 and the winter solstice of 2017. Gradually and steadily, you will change as a society, so that by 2027, you will have open contact with positive, benevolent beings from another world. It is still unclear who will be the first race or alliance to establish open contact with you. Currently, as we scan your timeline, beings from the Andromeda galaxy appear the most likely candidates. There is also an almost equally high probability that human-looking hybrids will be the first.

It is much more likely that the Liberation Forces will be the first to openly contact you. The Liberation Forces are a branch of benevolent extraterrestrials who engage in defensive combat. The Pleiadian Alliance is part of the Liberation Forces. We are an independent group and do not have "official" allies, but we do recognize other defensive groups interacting with you and we do assist each other from time to time. There are some benevolent extraterrestrial races who do not engage in war. These include many of the higher-dimensional beings who do not have physical bodies, as well as many spiritual groups who believe that war is never the answer. These non-combative groups are most likely to come second, in terms of open contact. The reason for this appears to be differences with regards to eagerness. The Liberation Forces are somewhat more eager, almost desperate, you could say, about interacting with you. The non-combative groups are generally more patient and appear to be in no hurry, at least from our point of view.

You will have visitors from many star systems, including the Pleiades, Sirius, Capella, Antares, Procyon, as well as many groups who do not have a home star system and simply wander the galaxy. You will begin to meet these beings on an individual and small-group basis beginning around the year 2019 or 2020. You will then have national and global contact around 2026. Rest assured that open contact will occur at a slow and steady rate. ETs are not going to rush in all at once. Your comfort and sanity is of high priority to us, and it is our intention to make open contact a sane and pleasant experience for you as best we can.

In addition to the alien visitors that are coming, you will also have some permanent residents who will live among you on Earth after their arrival, namely your hybrid children. As some of you know, a hybridization program is currently taking place on your world and has been active for several decades. Many abductees who report encounters with the beings you call the Greys are often aware of hybrid children that have spawned from genetic experiments with their DNA. Many of these hybrid children are eagerly anticipating direct interaction with their human mothers and fathers. This will be one of the most surprising wonders coming to your world. Many of you will have the opportunity to raise your extraterrestrial children right here on Earth!

Fourth Density

The universe is structured in layers, bands of frequencies that separate different levels of consciousness into different realities. There are twelve densities or layers of the universe that currently exist. The first density is that of basic matter – the atoms, molecules and particles, the grains of sand, fire, water, and air. The second level of consciousness are the life forms with limited, focused awareness. These are the bacteria, the insects, and the majority of animal species. They live mostly on instinct and can only comprehend the aspects of reality relative to their immediate, instinctual needs. The third level of consciousness are the life forms with limited, general awareness. They can comprehend the general framework of the reality around them, but are limited to an individuated and linear perception. This is where you exist. You are in the process of ascending from third density to fourth density.

In your Biblical stories, there are prophecies that foretell of a great Rapture – the ascension of humanity into the kingdom of heaven. The truth is that humanity is ascending into a higher plane of existence known as fourth density. It is not "heaven," per se. There is still a considerable amount of conflict and discomfort that can exist in fourth density. However, for many humans, the ascension process will undoubtedly be a heavenly experience indeed.

Once you cross the threshold into fourth density, you will find that any ailments, diseases, disabilities, and dysfunctions that afflict your body will suddenly disappear. You will shift into a shimmering, crystalline body with perfect health and vitality in the blink of an eye. This moment of ascension is the reason why so many souls have chosen to incarnate on Earth at this time. Seven billion souls, an unprecedented number, have incarnated at this point in time because the thrill of rapidly shifting from a 3D dark age reality into a 4D golden age reality is so exciting!

There are beings in higher dimensions who literally fight each other to the death for the chance to incarnate here. There is not enough room for everybody to incarnate all at once. Therefore, as you can imagine, many souls are frustrated and envious towards those who get to be here at this prestigious time on your planet. Some of you may think that living on Earth is a burden, a difficult challenge with little to no reward, but you'd be surprised at how many souls would give an arm and a leg to be in your place.

This grand transformative journey that you are undergoing has captured widespread galactic attention. It is very much akin to a butterfly, soaring beautifully out of its confining cocoon, or a phoenix bird rising brilliantly from the ashes. You can also think of it as a homeless man winning the lottery and shifting overnight from a degraded life of sorrow into a liberating life of luxury overnight. However you wish to picture it, the story of Earth is one of shifting quickly from great darkness into great light. We Pleiadians are confident that your ascension will be an astonishing, exhilarating experience you do not want to miss. We encourage you to stay grounded, stay poised, and be patience. We guarantee the rewards will be well worth the wait.

This phenomenon of ascension is not exclusive to humanity. Entire planets and life forms ascend or descend through densities all the time. Just as the universe has many layers of itself, so too do the stars and planets. For example, in your third density reality, your planet Venus appears uninhabited, yet it is teeming with intelligent life in its fourth density version. Sometimes, a planet's higher density can be very similar to one of its lower layers, and other times it can be radically different. There is also the process of descension. Your human race was once a fifth density civilization during the legendary time of Atlantis, yet as you lowered your frequency and fell deeper into materialism, you descending down into 4D and eventually further down into 3D. This descension process from 5D to 3D took about one thousand years to complete and occurred approximately 13 thousand years ago in your history.

Nonetheless, you are ascending once again and will return to fifth density reality, but first you must cross through the transitory level of fourth density. You have already begun the ascension process and it will become more apparent in your year of 2017 or 2018. The human population will begin to experience the physical symptoms of ascension. There is high probability that you will slowly begin to recall past-life memories, as well as dream state or out-of-body memories, during this time frame. You are also likely to experience increased telepathy, empathy, and psychic connection with both physical and spirit beings around you. The pineal gland, which is literally a third eye in your brain with photoreceptive properties, will begin to activate. These symptoms will be the result of genetic codes that have been shut down and are now toggling back on.

We have noticed a lot of talk about the mental symptoms of ascension, but your spiritual communities rarely talk about the physical changes that are coming. Dear friends, it is our pleasure to share with you the coming changes to your physical bodies. Just as your brain and pineal gland will begin to upgrade and ascend toward fourth density reality, so too will the rest of your body. One particular aspect we wish to talk about is your immune systems.

The Anunnaki are a race of extraterrestrial beings that came to your world approximately 300 thousand years ago. They genetically altered the indigenous race of humanoids that existed at that time to create the first wave of humans on Earth. When they infused their DNA and genetic material with the indigenous race, they effectively bestowed upon them a great deal of physiological features, strengths, and abilities. One notable aspect of Anunnaki genetics is their robust immune systems. The Anunnaki are practically immune to all diseases and ailments known to man. They are biotechnology experts and have used their advanced skills to fortify their immune systems into peak physical condition. You carry these genetic programs within you.

As more and more of your DNA begins to activate in this window we call the Splitting Prism of Time, your immune system will become more like the Anunnaki's. We cannot list every change you having coming, but we can assure you that your physical body will begin to upgrade on all levels, including the brain and pineal gland. This is especially exciting for humans with disabilities, for we see that the blind will gradually regain their vision, the paralyzed will regain their mobility, the overweight will regain their metabolism, the mentally ill will regain their stability, etc. The ascension process, as it activates more of your dormant Anunnaki DNA will literally heal and rejuvenate your entire body!

The time frame for ascension in which you will experience yourselves as a full-fledged fourth density being is between the years of 2020 and 2025. This is why we suggested applying the number "2020" to the title of this book because this is the first year with enough potential to shift you into fourth density consciousness. However, the highest probability for ascension, as we gauge your collective energy now, is not until 2021 or 2022. The more each of you keep your emotions high and your thoughts positive, the sooner this grand transition can occur. Integrating and developing a more loving connection with each other is the key – the more positive you become, the more your physical reality will follow.

Now, we wish to offer further explanation of fourth density reality. This layer of the universe is not a utopia, just to be frank. There is very much the potential for pain and suffering in this plane; you will still be physical beings, after all. There will still be a need for doctors and healers on your world because even though you will start your 4D experience with perfect health, it is still possible to manifest injury and physical stress thereafter. The Pleiadian Alliance exists in fourth density, and we can attest that there is much war and conflict that exists here. It may not be as common or as intense as it is in 3D, but the point we wish to make is that fourth density is not a positive experience for everyone who lives here. So, if you have a passion for healing and helping others, do not feel discouraged. There are many souls who can use a helping hand in this plane of existence. We, as a defensive military alliance, would not exist here otherwise. There is much healing that is needed throughout fourth density reality.

Additionally, we wish to explain the general experience of living in fourth density. As you climb the dimensional ladder, you will become more spirit-based. Meaning, you can operate more like a spirit being. When you exist as a fully non-physical being with pure spirit consciousness, there are no limitations – your wish is Creation's command. Just like in a lucid dream where you can conjure up entire events and realities simply by the power of your thoughts, so too can you operate in this manner in the spirit realms.

As third density beings, you are 100% physical. In fourth density, you will become 75% physical. The remaining 25% of your being will be made of pure spirit essence. In other words, you will have 25% the capacity to operate as a spirit being in fourth density! That means 25% the abilities and freedom of a spirit will be yours. Then, as you enter fifth density, you will become even less physical. In fifth density, physicality constitutes only 50% of reality. This is why fifth density is the most popular and most populated density of all. The majority of souls throughout the universe enjoy the half-and-half state of fifth density, for it offers challenges without them being too easy or too difficult. You can think of fifth density as the "Goldilocks' zone" of the universe where conditions are not too hot or too cold – they are "just right," for most souls anyway. There are some who do prefer the higher densities and some who prefer the lower. You will reach fifth density reality, the biggest funhouse or playground of the universe, in time.

Your crystalline fourth density body will be much different than the body you have now. Your brain will operate much quicker, your muscles will be able to lift heavier weights, you will be able to run faster. Of course, you will also weigh less. You will eat less and sleep less. In fourth density, most beings only require 2 to 3 hours of sleep. Also, your body will no longer produce waste material. Food is converted into 100% energy at the 4D level, so you will no longer excrete bodily waste of any kind. The most exciting difference between your 3D and 4D bodies to us is your nervous system. Currently, your body carries more receptors for pain than for pleasure. You make countless horror movies that capitalize on the severity of pain your bodies can induce. In 4D, this will no longer be the case. You will become less sensitive to pain while becoming more sensitive to pleasure and beauty, both physically and emotionally. We applaud this tremendously!

Time becomes nonexistent at the multidimensional level because, going back to the magnifying glass analogy, you can see that everything exists all at once, and you can literally be in all places at once. The higher you climb the dimensional ladder, the more you will become spirit-like in nature. In fourth density reality, your perception of space and time will be different. In general, you will find that time is more flexible, not set in stone. You will have some conscious ability to move slightly forward or backward in time, as you perceive time. For example, if you are 15 minutes late for an appointment, you might find yourself arriving just in time despite whatever obstacles. Or if you think you are arriving too early for a party, you might find yourself arriving just in time as well. Time will adhere to your will, to some degree, more so than it does now in 3D. Time operates with greater synchronicity in fourth density.

One interesting prediction we would like to make for this ascension process is that psychics, mediums, and channelers will be out of business by 2027. By this year, all of you will be full-fledged psychics. There will be no need to turn to another human for psychic insight or guidance because you will have your own psychic link to the cosmos and your spirit guides. The only ones who will require psychic counseling will be children and other individuals whose psychic senses have not fully developed or who need assistance in understanding their psychic perceptions. Most of you will become psychically independent, able to read energetic currents and impressions with clear analysis.

Telepathy is a whole new level of communication. When your race becomes telepathic, you will discover various new ways of interacting with each other. There are telepathic ways to be mischievous, flirtatious, loud, quiet, humorous, etc. For example, within The Pleiadian Alliance, in moments of rest or "break time," we might attempt to amuse each other with acts of trickery. One basic example is we might verbally tell someone to go left while telepathically telling them to go right. We find causing this type of confusion very humorous. Another example, a man might radiate a telepathic signal that attempts to convince others he is an animal, or a chair, or a female. We trick and tease each other like this all the time.

You will discover exciting new ways of playing with one another as you become more telepathic.

Also, as result of becoming more psychic, you will find that death due to natural disasters will be greatly diminished by 2025. Throughout the universe, it is common for creatures in a positive reality to have a psychic rapport with their mother planet. They can communicate with her and are in tune with her energetic currents at all times. If an earthquake or hurricane is brewing, they can sense it and move out of the way before it strikes. There many myths on your world about the psychic nature of animals. Many reports tell of radical instinctual behavior that animals display prior to an imminent disaster. It is no secret that animals are more psychic than humans. As more genetic upgrades occur, you will find yourselves becoming much more intuitive like your animal counterparts. In time, all of Earth's creatures will be psychically in tune with her. When you start noticing yourself and others having an increasing, instinctual connection with Mother Earth, you will know the golden age is coming.

Due to the rise of psychic abilities and telepathic experiences on your planet, we believe there will be much chaos and confusion that will arise. 2017 and 2018 will be years of great adventure for some while being years of outrage for others. Those who do not wish to see the truth, to see beyond the veil, who wish to stay within limited 3D perceptions in order to maintain their power or status will become very upset. Once these highly conservative individuals begin to see those around themselves transcending the old beliefs and traditions, they will exert violence in an attempt to suppress the ascending world around them. This brings us to the next subject we wish to talk about...

Terrorism and War

The lower chakras are responsible for all acts of war on your planet. Since ego-driven individuals are interested in superiority rather than equality, domination by war is a common practice within negative realities. There is an interesting phenomenon that can arise from this – positive individuals, those with an egalitarian mindset, are sometimes possessed by the energy of war. When positive individuals engage in defensive combat, they sometimes succumb to the thrill of power and destruction, and thus, they themselves become negative. Engaging in defensive combat can be very dangerous. The allure of power is a great temptation, one that many souls fail to resist. A spiritual warrior must be a master at self-discipline in order to retain compassion and not get carried away by the power-hungry, self-indulging temptations of the ego.

The Pleiadian Alliance has lost hundreds of warriors to temptation. In fact, in our alliance, our members are more likely to cross over to the dark side than to die in battle. Due to our level of technology and centuries of training, we seldom lose warriors in combat. At the moment, there are a few members who concern me. I fear they may succumb to temptation like so many others have. I know of a few members who even place bets on other members, gambling over who will convert next. Since our alliance, like most positive alliances, is volunteer-based, we have no means of preventing or stopping a person from converting to the dark side. Without going into much detail, I can say that I've lost my youngest brother to temptation. He is now working for an enemy group. I still wake from sleep some days in anticipation, hoping today will be the day that he returns to us. I am unable to determine if he ever will.

Because the ego chakra overshadows a substantial portion of consciousness in your current reality, it will require many years before the momentum behind it begins to considerably die down. We are strongly sensing an explosive finale, the war to end all wars, so to speak, coming soon to your world. This will not incite a third world war. We wish to be very clear on that. Instead, what we perceive is a major terrorist attack targeting American soil. There is no guarantee that this will occur, but there is high probability and momentum behind it. It will be akin to your September 11 incident, only several times greater in scale and magnitude. Both nuclear and chemical weapons will most likely be used. It will impact several cities across the United States, from the east coast to the west coast. Simply put, it will be a day of fire and booms for the USA. This probability is likely to unfold around your year of 2018.

As we stated, this will be the war to end all wars. In a sense, this will be the final shot fired. This incident will shock and awaken humans to the recognition that war is no longer an interest that your collective has. Wealthy conservatives will vocalize their desire for world war, as can be expected, but Americans will be aware enough by this point to know that war only makes the rich richer and the poor poorer, and with new-found restrictions on governmental power by this time, military retaliation of any sort will not be permitted. Any leaders advocating war will be met with mass public backlash.

Whether this probable event unfolds or not, you will establish peace on Earth one way or another. Eventually, an uprising against production of nuclear weapons will occur. Humanity will begin to realize that weapons of mass destruction are only used for regressive, self-destructive purposes. People will demand and implement a steering away from the investing of billions of dollars on military power. As Pleiadians, we believe that the most peaceful solution to war, in any situation, is to disarm the enemy. Many of our historical figures have ended wars by this mere tactic alone. Therefore, what we are foreseeing is a curtailing of military power across the globe, including the Middle East. In time, all nations will put down their guns, and by your year of 2027, you will find that mass-scale acts of terrorism and war will cease to exist.

Medical Breakthroughs

Disease is another trademark of negative realities. Within hierarchical, all-for-one societies, it is quite common for the healthiest, most vital bodies to be occupied by a select number of souls while the majority of souls are burdened with bodies that are prone to varying levels of dysfunction and disease. Again, one cannot experience itself as powerful or superior unless all else are inferior by comparison. From our point of view, condemning a soul to the constant pains and frustrations of a crippled body is one of the most inhumane practices we have ever witnessed. Your governmental overlords have played with a myriad of different ways to keep your general population sick and dependent on money-grubbing drug companies. This of course is not suitable for a golden age.

Dear friends, let us be the first to tell you, there is a natural remedy, and sometimes cure, for almost every ailment that exists on your planet. Earth is the most prestigious botanical garden, the most medicine-rich biosphere we have ever encountered. Over the last 300,000 years, countless races have contributed to the vast collection of plants that dwell here. Though the information is currently suppressed, we assure you that these plants can alter your physiological chemistry in virtually every conceivable way. When the time is appropriate, according to your collective agreements, you will discover natural cures and treatments for every disease that afflicts your population.

Our main prediction for your medical industry is a revolution of sincerity. Currently, your medical industry is mostly interested in amassing wealth. This will begin to change somewhat during the Splitting Prism of Time. However, we do not see a radical change in medical practices until about 2019. Between now and then, there will likely be upgraded versions of medical treatments that already exist. It is also possible that some major diseases will be cured. We believe that 2017 may see the cure for cancer. However, this is not for certain until 2019.

The key to any health treatment, no matter the condition, is frequency control. When you learn to focus electromagnetic waves in specific, computer-guided directions so that they target only the body parts being treated while leaving everything else untouched, you can work miracles. Your biological bodies are chemical masses. Learning how to alter the electromagnetic mass of chemistry that is your body is the key to every health issue. Medical technology that can precisely diagnose and alter the chemistry of your bodies can emerge as early as 2023, as we scan your timeline. This can emerge sooner or later, depending on your actions and decisions.

One interesting bit of medical technology that The Pleiadian Alliance uses is called "revert technology." In the same way that many of you are able to revert your home computer back to an earlier time before it became infected with viruses or malware, we too are able to revert our bodies back to a previous version. The machine we use to facilitate this procedure is like a large coffin that scans and records the entire chemistry of a person's body. If the person becomes ill or badly injured, what we can do is place them inside this coffin-shaped machine and electromagnetically rewire their physiological chemistry so that it matches a previous recording of their body when it was perfectly healthy and whole. Humanity is decades away from having this sort of technology, but we are confident you will get there someday.

Despite the fact that your Anunnaki DNA will take your health to superhuman heights by 2025, humans will still create somewhat negative situations for themselves and thus require teams of doctors and healers for years to come. And as you enter fourth density reality and realize the creative power of your thoughts and emotions more so, spirituality and science will merge into one. Not only will scientific advances introduce new methods of curing physical ailments, but the mental and emotional underlying roots of the problem will be addressed as well. Humanity will discover that mental and emotional clarity is an essential part of preventative care and general well-being. Spirituality and physicality are inseparable.

Sexuality

Throughout the cosmos, sex is one of the most popular pursuits. We have observed that sex often catalyzes strong spiritual bonds between souls. We have also observed that exposure to sex often results in abandonment of spirituality and addiction to physical sensations. These observations are bewildering to us. The sexual union of your body with another being can either be your greatest sense of spiritual connection or disconnection. There are both positive and negative uses for sex throughout the universe.

On your planet, sexuality is in dire need of healing. During the time of Atlantis, sex was based on mutual pleasure. The Atlanteans practiced "free love," a polyamorous lifestyle that allowed individuals to mate with many partners without judgment or jealously. Though marriages were still common practice, open marriages were the norm. Humans expressed love and attraction without being culturally restricted to only one partner or gender. Because the Atlanteans were telepathic, sex was more than just for physical pleasure and procreation; it was about the exchange of psychic information and soul communication as well.

You, as a race, have steered far away from this integrative and wholesome lifestyle over the last six thousand years. You have spiraled into cultural and genetic programming that imposes many restrictions on your sexuality. This dark-age version of sexuality is designed to leave the majority of humans in frustration. The majority of men on your planet have a sex drive that is built for a harem owner. To indulge and revolve their lives around sex is a compelling passion held by many men on your world. Of course, the majority of men cannot achieve the pornographic lifestyle they desire. Women, on the other hand, are often burdened with sexual frustrations of a different nature. They are burdened with bleeding, low sex drive, discomfort during intercourse and anguish during childbirth. While a majority of men on your world are built for sexual addiction, women are built for sexual discomfort and shame, especially in your eastern cultures.

Also, a large portion of men on your world are genetically programmed to be sexually responsive only to women with physical features that meet the cultural standards for beauty. A large portion of women, on the other hand, are programmed to be attracted primarily to men with high status and wealth. Both men and women on your planet experience a high degree of sexual shallowness, where relationships are commonly based on fulfilling the lower chakras of survival and self-gratification while ignoring the upper chakras of spiritual unity and enlightenment.

This of course is not suitable for a golden age. As we scan your probable future, we can assure you that relationships and sexuality on your planet look much brighter than they do now. What we see coming is an expansion of sexuality occurring at the individual and collective level. As you move further into the ascension process, you may find yourself attracted to body types, personalities, identities, and lifestyles that you previously did not desire. You will not lose the sexuality that you currently have, you will simply experience an expansion of it, a broadening of what you perceive to be attractive. And we applaud this – the more the merrier, we say. You will begin to fall in love with people that you could not fall in love with before, and people who could not love you before will suddenly begin to fall in love you as well. You are moving back to Atlantean sexuality, where you can fall in love with the majority of people, not just a handful.

This blossoming of sexuality will take time, of course. The human genome requires much activation. The beginnings of this expansion will become readily apparent in your 2020s and will become the cultural norm by the end of your 2030s. For those of you who feel resistant, triggered, and disappointed by this information, it may serve you to know there will still be individuals who prefer a life of strict monogamy. Though it is often a trademark of negative, limited societies, there are positive societies throughout the universe that practice monogamy as well. Within The Pleiadian Alliance, many of our members are in monogamous relationships. If monogamy is your heart's truest desire, rest assured that there will be a place for you in the new golden age. However, as more and more humans awaken and embrace the coming free love movement, you may find yourself in a romantic wonderland where love and connection are more abundant than ever before, and this may be very tempting.

Another trademark of negative realities is sexual superiority and dominance by one gender over the other. Currently, sexual encounters on your world often grant orgasm for the male while denying orgasm to the female. Most men on your planet experience hundreds of orgasms by the time they are 20 years old while some women go their entire lives without experiencing even one. There is also widespread raping of females by males on your world, especially at the underground level. These iniquities are typical of a negative society. This must change. You must bring yourselves into wholesome balance. During the time of Atlantis, mutual respect and mutual pleasure were the norm, and we are delighted to say that they will be the norm once again.

You are living in patriarchal times. Throughout many spiritual communities, dark ages are regarded as masculine ages, whereas golden ages are regarded as feminine ages. From our perspective, this is inaccurate. In order for a dark age to thrive, it requires both masculine/aggressive and feminine/passive individuals. On your planet, the majority of the population is passive/submissive. This allows a minority of self-serving individuals to outshine and dominate the majority. Therefore, a golden age is not about emphasizing femininity or masculinity; it is about the balance of both. You must realize that these battles you keep waging upon yourselves are detrimental – masculine versus feminine, intellect versus intuition, service-to-self versus service-to-others... Understand, dear friends, that only harmonious balance between polarities is what creates a positive experience or reality.

If you are service-to-others oriented and you encounter someone that is service-to-self, guess what? You wind up servicing that person while receiving little to no service in return. You are out of balance. You must learn to become both service-to-others and service-to-self equally. Do not be aggressive or passive, which are both negative orientations. Learn to be assertive, the positive balance of both. Embrace the coming changes that will improve your disposition. We cannot stress this enough.

Because most of you have the notion that dark ages tend to be masculine and patriarchal, we wish to share a brief story with you. Our records show that you have cycled through at least 3 golden ages and dark ages over the last 300,000 years. During the previous dark age you experienced, it was women who ruled the Earth. Currently, the patriarchal conditions of your societies are introduced by a race of extraterrestrial invaders known as the Reptilians. These lizard-like beings come primarily from the Orion and Alpha Draconis star systems. During the previous dark age, more than 50,000 years ago, the invading extraterrestrials were a race of malicious, highly intelligent, humanoid arachnidans. These beings are a much larger, much more advanced version of the spiders that exist on your planet. They come from star systems located in the Scorpio constellation. It is no coincidence that you assign certain names to certain star systems; you subconsciously know what dwells there.

The upper class of Arachnidans are humanoids with four arms, two legs, six eyes, and two large, retractable fangs. The lower class of Arachnidans tend to be a more degraded, less intelligent version that appear like giant black widows the size of your automobiles. All the Arachnidan races we've observed can create web traps and are notorious for blood farming their captives. These malevolent creatures tend to form matriarchies. They introduced a brutal matriarchal society on your planet long ago that practiced mass cannibalism of men. It was during this time that men experienced tremendous oppression, where they were regarded as nothing more than expendable workers and food. The trauma accumulated from this dark age explains the prominent fear of spiders held by most of the human population – the memories are still lingering in your DNA.

The power pendulum of humanity has swung back and forth between men and women many times throughout your history. You come into harmonious balance for approximately 20,000 years and then slowly spiral out of balance into 5,000 years of patriarchal or matriarchal darkness where one gender dominates the other. These cycles have repeated many times, but the glorious truth is that your current dark age will be the last. Because the Earth has become the universal center of attention, it will be impossible for malevolent races to invade your planet once you've allied yourselves with the countless interstellar alliances that await your membership. Your level of protection, power, spirituality, and freedom will go beyond the reach of any hostile being. From our point of view, the upcoming golden age looks promising as a permanent paradise on Earth.

We wish to address reproduction for a moment. Throughout the cosmos, reproduction happens in a variety of ways. This includes both sexual and asexual methods. Currently, on your planet, reproduction is very painful experience. It was not always this way. In most positive societies, the birthing experience is often accompanied with orgasm or euphoria; it is rewarded, not punished. In negative societies, however, it is often accompanied with pain, blood, and sometimes death. Depending on the dominant gender, the oppressed gender in a negative reality is often condemned to painful intercourse and either painful ejaculations for men or painful childbirth for women. These are tell-tell signs of a negative reality.

The genetic codes for orgasmic birth are carried by every female on the planet. Less than 1% of human women can currently experience this. These genes are recessive and the codes for painful birth are much more dominant. Some women have reported pleasurable birth experiences. This will become the norm as you ascend further into fourth density, where your Atlantean DNA will resurface and serve as the foundation for the Alpha Human. This will become apparent by 2019 as women report orgasmic birth experiences in growing numbers. Between 2020 and 2025, you may find yourself donning a 4D, crystalline body that no longer supports negative systems of the old days. Mothers of all species on Earth will experience the giving of life as a beautiful, rewarding experience. Childbearing may likely return to its former glory, where mother and child undergo spiritual bonding accompanied by euphoric sensations that expand the mind and elevate the spirit in the most celebratory moments of motherhood.

You are in the process of converting from a dysfunctional species into a functional species. Just you as label your families and relationships on Earth as functional or dysfunctional, we have observed entire species and races that are functional or dysfunctional. The difference between your species and other dysfunctional species throughout the cosmos is that you have the potential to change. You carry exceptionally advanced genetic makeup within your bodies. With proper frequency modulation, your so-called "junk" DNA can be activated, like a light switch toggling from off to on. This is not possible for many species outside your solar system. In order for us to help some negative societies transmute themselves, we must reprogram their DNA completely by adding new genetic codes that were not already present.

Just as the Reptilians and other malevolent forces have altered your DNA to render you dysfunctional and controllable, we Pleiadians have altered many species throughout the galaxy to render them functional, enlightened and free. This of course must always be done with their consent. We communicate and appeal to their higher selves, often their astral selves during sleep time, and we establish consensual agreements to assist them. It's an arduous task, but the more positive we become as a galaxy, as a universe, the better our chances at ensuring a sovereign future for all of us.

Death

Death is an important topic for us to address. When most people on your world die, they often die in fear and confusion. They're soul is disoriented upon exiting the body. This disorientation renders you vulnerable and susceptible to manipulation by dark forces. Instead of remembering your true identity and returning to Oneness or your oversoul, or reincarnating to a more positive reality, most of you find yourselves returning to Earth over and over again for another life of heavy challenges. Though you do reincarnate into positions of power and freedom from time to time, most of your incarnations on Earth are into positions of mediocrity or inferiority. The ignorance about life after death, what to do, where to go upon leaving the body is part of the mechanism which keeps human souls trapped on this planet.

The key to a wholesome, healthy death experience is wisdom. The more you understand the astral plane and the nature of spirit realms, the less disoriented you will be when the time comes to depart from your body. We've observed many religions that attempt to manipulate your understanding of the afterlife. In reality, the afterlife is not about meeting demons in a fiery hell or angels in a cloudy heaven. The afterlife is an experience that each of you have, an opportunity to detach from physicality. Sometimes you wish to reincarnate (you may not be consciously aware of it, but you choose to reincarnate in order to clear karmic ties). Other times, you choose to leave and return to your oversoul in the 7th dimension, or sometimes you return to total Oneness.

There is no standard path for life after death. Every soul has the potential to create something unique. Unfortunately, the majority of human souls are conditioned to create similar scenarios upon death. The majority of you experience the famous tunnel of light that guides you to an Earth-life paradise. You stay in this paradise very briefly, just long enough to be shown a life review and then be persuaded into returning to physical life on Earth. Some humans are even conditioned to believe that they will burn for all eternity after death.

The Pleiadian Alliance has observed many dark, hellish realities since its formation. Your Earth and the dark age you are cycling through is relatively benign compared to other infernos we've encountered. However, no matter the depth of darkness, the degree of pain, the level of ignorance and disempowerment in any reality, we have never observed eternal damnation. This just comes to show the power of each soul's will. The purpose of Creation is to experience reality from all possible perspectives. Therefore, by definition, it is impossible for you to stay in one particular reality forever. You are bound to change perspectives sooner or later. Even if a painful situation appears to last for eons, there is always the return to neutrality and Oneness. There is no such thing as eternal damnation.

We foresee many improvements in your approach to death and the afterlife. By the year 2022, the majority of humans will be contacted by spirit beings in one way or another. As your third eye opens, you will begin to realize that the spirit realm truly does exist. A minority of humans can already peer into other dimensions. Mediumship becomes much more prevalent in the coming years. Skepticism falls into obsoleteness by 2025. The fear of dying subsides considerably by this point, and because of your newfound multidimensional awareness, you will be able to astral project at will and leave your body with clarity and grace, having total control of your passage from one dimension to another.

Alpha Earth

There are an infinite number of parallel realities that exist. Every conceivable variation of a person, place, or thing exists somewhere within Creation. The Earth has an infinity of parallel variations as well. The version of Earth that we can perceive as being the highest in terms of quality and frequency is the version we refer to as Alpha Earth. This version of Earth is a masterpiece in comparison to all other versions. We liken it to the most wonderful, the most enchanting fairy tale you can imagine.

We want you to think of a movie that strikes your fancy, a movie that you consider to be high quality. Think about how perfect the dialogue is, how smooth the timing is, how artistic the scenery is, how emotional the music is, etc. Think of a masterpiece. You are literally shifting from a reality that is generally lackluster into a reality that is a golden masterpiece. This is our prophecy for you, humans. This will become visibly apparent as the architecture of your cities begin to change.

Currently, your architecture reflects patriarchy. As we have observed throughout the universe, the architecture of male or intellect-dominated societies tends to be mostly squared or rectangular. Notice the shape of houses and buildings on your planet – nearly everything looks like a box. This is very telling of a predominantly masculine or intellect-dominated society. During the time of Atlantis, buildings featured a greater display of spirals and spheres. There was also a greater emphasis on artistic lighting and ambience. These designs are often reflective of feminine or heart-centered realities. As we look into your future, we can see the architecture of your cities, and we are dazzled! The architecture of

Alpha Earth looks like artistry inspired straight from a fantasy drawing where the land appears decorated in dreamy colors and the buildings appear like enchanted castles of various shapes and sizes.

Some of you may not know how creative you are. For thousands of years, Earth has been a place where creative souls from all over the galaxy and universe are banished here as prisoners. There are many political powers throughout the universe that use Earth as a prison planet, and so as punishment for being creative, for being passionate about singing, acting, writing, painting, etc., these creative souls are banished to Earth to live lives filled with heavy challenges. Our galaxy, the Milky Way, is predominantly patriarchal and there is much persecution against beings who are creative or feminine in their interests and expressions.

Because Earth has been a dumping ground for so many creative souls, your world is one giant pot of creative talent, all buried and suppressed under political, patriarchal power. Think for a moment, dear friends. Imagine how brilliant the creativity on this planet will be once the bird is let out of the cage. Imagine how explosive all that artistic energy will be once it is allowed to flourish and thrive. When your creative abilities are set free, as an entire species, you will usher in the Alpha Earth, and a time of great enchantment, of incredible entertainment will dawn. It is only a matter of time. You are approaching the party of a cosmic lifetime! The entire universe wants to be here.

We wish to clarify that you will each retain a distinct personality. Each of you will continue to play a distinctive role within the living play that is your world. Because of diversity, there will be those who will continue to play rather secondary roles, and some who will continue to play rather antagonistic roles. This does not mean that anyone will suffer, per se. You will continue to create social and physical challenges for yourselves, but rather than those challenges being unsurmountable or mundane, they will instead be stimulating and entertaining. After all, what is a masterpiece without an engaging problem and a satisfying solution? What we are saying is that Alpha Earth will not be a utopia in the classical sense. You will continue taking turns in stimulating each other with drama and elements of contrast.

Knowledge is power. Therefore, a dark age is an age of ignorance, whereas a golden age is an age of wisdom. Currently, you are shrouded in mystery. You question your true history and wonder how you got here. After the burning of the Library of Alexandria on your world, you erased invaluable knowledge about your origins and the nature of existence. You must regain this knowledge in order to progress into the new golden age. What we sense, as we scan your timeline, is the discovery of ancient documents that contain most of your true history. This information is most likely to emerge from Egypt around 2020. As you integrate and process this information, you will regain your memories of Atlantis and establish a new age of enlightenment on Earth.

It is no coincidence that the year 2020 or 2021 marks the birth of generation A, or alpha. The previous generations were named X, Y, and Z. You are now returning back to the first letter of the alphabet. You are wiping the slate clean and initiating a fresh new start. The alpha generation will be very special. Generations Y and Z were the first generations to introduce new open-minded ways of thinking. They are responsible for the resurgence of liberalism in your society. Generation A will not only raise human consciousness to higher levels, they will also be born with a substantial amount of active DNA. Spiritual wisdom will be inherent to their being, and the majority of them will incarnate directly into fourth density with full-fledged awareness and abilities that have not been present on your world since the time of Atlantis. It is at the time of their arrival that the Alpha Earth golden age may begin.

The key to a successful dark age is self-destruction. The worst way to destroy an individual is to turn the individual against him or herself. Currently, the majority of you humans are born into genetic and societal circumstances that render you self-destructive. Most of you experience self-hatred to some degree for one reason or another. The more you condemn yourself for being unattractive, untalented, unintelligent, unsuccessful, etc., the more you block your flow of energy and impose negative synchronicities or "bad luck" upon yourselves. When you dislike someone, you tend to avoid or antagonize that person, and when you dislike yourself, you can just as easily become your own worst enemy. By not loving your mind, body, and soul, you are self-defeated.

Generation Alpha will not be born into such self-destructive circumstances. They will not be as prone to self-hatred and self-defeat as most of you are. Because of this, they will create higher amounts of positive synchronicities or "good luck" for themselves. This will mark the dramatic switch of your planetary status from negative to positive. These children, born in 2020 or 2021, will anchor very high positive energies so that positive beings from other realities can interact with your world by law of attraction, by frequency match.

Your identity will change dramatically in fourth density. Currently, many of you have self-love and self-worth issues. You judge and criticize yourselves harshly because you are unhappy with the body and/or personality you carry. Believe us when we say, there will still be vast amounts of diversity on Alpha Earth. You will not become identical, homogeneous clones of one another with ideal male or female qualities like Adam and Eve. You will all become ideal in your own unique way.

In terms of beauty, we wish to emphasize that yes you will all be physically beautiful and attractive in 4D, but not in the way that most of you assume. Currently, you regard only certain people with specific facial and bodily proportions to be beautiful. That will not be the case in 4D. As we have said, as more of your DNA activates, your standards and perceptions of beauty will expand. So, if you look into the mirror and think to yourself that the shape of your nose is appalling, you might find that from your 4D perspective, that same nose will suddenly appear flawless. You can think of yourself as being currently limited or blind to beauty. You have very strict limitations as to what you can register as physically beautiful, but as your senses expand, you will discover beauty in things you never noticed before. Ultimately, all humans will be considered attractive, and no one will be denied affection, intimacy, or love.

We understand the challenges you face, humans. We are here to encourage you. Continue moving forward. We guarantee there is a light at the end of the tunnel, and you are on the verge of reaching that light, that long-awaited freedom. Your soul is not masochistic. You did not incarnate here to suffer without compensation or a worthwhile reward. There is always karmic balance. We assure you that the pains you experience are necessary for the exhilarating joy you are about to experience. It is very much like being out in the cold, shivering and trembling in discomfort – the colder you feel, the more soothing and rewarding a dip in warm water feels by comparison, does it not? The impact of the brilliant light you are reaching would not be so striking and mind-blowing if not for contrast of the cold and bitter darkness. Your arduous wait will be worth it, and you will prevail. This is the path your collective consciousness has chosen, in unison with the universal consciousness, and it is your destiny to emerge from the ashes as a race of sovereign beings with exceptional abilities. By definition, in a supreme golden age, all beings must be loved, empowered, and free. And so you shall be.

The 13ᵗʰ Dimension

The universe is birthing a new dimension, a new density. The 12th dimension is the highest level of consciousness, where you experience yourself as all that exists within the universe. There will come a time when you will reach this level. The identity and experiences of everyone and everything within the universe will be yours. This includes anyone you have ever interacted with; you are them and they are you. By the highly focused nature of your mind, however, you are not aware of being all that exists at this time.

The 13th dimension is largely unknown and mysterious to us. The bits of data we have managed to collect indicates this dimension to be a direct bridge between our universe and the multiverse. It will be a dimension of partial multiversal consciousness. However, the multiverse is infinitely vast, and there is no telling what region of the multiverse our universe will connect with.

What we do know is that the 13th dimension will determine the fate of the universe. It will allow easy passage between us and beings from other universes. The birth of this dimension is happening in synchronicity with relation to the affairs of Earth. The nexus of the universe is the deciding factor in whether we bridge the gap between a dark region of the multiverse or a region of beauty and light.

Ultimately, The Creator will experience both outcomes and every parallel version of those outcomes. However, we in the present now moment have the option to choose the path we most desire. If we choose the path of light, we may experience a revamping of the entire universe that can benefit the majority of souls. Though it may require eons of work, we may find ourselves free to renovate the universe to our liking. The legion of entities possessed by the ego chakra may lessen. The majority of souls in our relatively young universe may be able to experience innocence and playfulness in safety, without being constantly pestered by beings with selfish intents. From the Alpha Earth, an alpha version of our shared universe can emerge. Together we can co-create a journey toward a universe that transcends all other versions.

I, ambassador of The Pleiadian Alliance, wish to thank you and all incarnates on Earth, the Crown of the Cosmos. We feel privileged to communicate with you and are grateful for your acceptance. There are countless other stories we look forward to sharing with you. We are confident this encounter will not be our last.

One final note we wish to leave you with is a final prediction, a prophecy – as humanity ascends into higher consciousness, the time will come, approximately 200 years from now, when you advance enough to venture out into space, we foresee you sharing your wisdom with beings throughout the universe. Though you might be unaware of it, many of you are actually in training to become galactic, spiritual teachers. The majority of extraterrestrial guides, including we Pleiadians, have not experienced the extreme highs and lows that humanity has. As you integrate the knowledge accumulated from your various lifetimes, you will rise from the ashes having unmatched empathy with beings from all walks of life, all personalities and polarities. We are speaking to students who will become some of the greatest and most legendary teachers of the universe. And this excites us very much.

-Deltavash

Conclusion

Thank you for reading my book. For those of you who may be wondering, I have chosen to remain anonymous. Therefore, I will not share my contact information or make myself available for public events. The experiences I have when connecting with my spirit guides are always very private and personal to me, and I wish to keep it that way. I am not interested in becoming a public figure and I deeply apologize if this disappoints anyone.

I decided to share these automatic writings because I felt they would inspire others. I sincerely hope I have accomplished that. I believe it is important for us to share uplifting information with one another, but without becoming dependent. When we become dependent on others for spiritual information, we neglect our inner knowings. It may serve us to be guided by others from time to time, but the best answers to our grand questions about life are always found inside our own minds and hearts.

If you enjoyed these messages from my spirit guide Deltavash and The Pleiadian Alliance, please feel free to share and spread the word. The more we focus on a positive future, the higher our chance of creating it. I truly believe that a bright new world is underway and that each of us are contributing to bringing forth that golden reality in one way or another. No matter how big or small our impact on the world around us can be, it is important to take action in raising the collective frequency as best we can.

As Deltavash has stated, the transformation of our planet from negative to positive begins with us. By donning a more assertive personality, by interacting with each other on the basis of mutual respect and mutual pleasure, we can become a functional species that integrates the polarities of male and female. A world society based on equality, vitality and liberty for all is within our reach. The power to change the planet and affect the entire universe is carried by every one of us. That power lies within you.

-James Carwin

CPSIA information can be obtained
at www.ICGtesting.com
Printed in the USA
LVHW052341261018
594934LV00001B/2/P